TOURING THE PEAK DISTRICT AND DERBYSHIRE BY CAR

by
John N. Merrill

Maps and Photographs by John N. Merrill

A JNM PUBLICATION

A J.N.M. PUBLICATION

JNM PUBLICATIONS, WINSTER, MATLOCK, DERBYSHIRE, DE4 2DQ.

Conceived, edited, typeset and designed by John N. Merrill.

© Text and Routes—John N. Merrill 1986.

© Maps and Photographs—John N. Merrill 1986.

First published 1974 as Motoring in Derbyshire,

Reprinted 1983, 1984 (twice)

This revised edition July 1986.

ISBN No. 0 907496 22 9

Typesetting interfaced by: Steve Rothwell Typesetting Services,
20 St. Ann's Square, Manchester, M2 7HG.

fount: Goudy Oldstyle Oldstyle Italic & Bold
point size: Headings 22 point text 11 point
line space: 11½ point

Printed by: Castle Harrod, Coalville, Leicestershire.

J.N.M. Publications, Winster, Matlock, Derbyshire, DE4 2DQ.

Cover photograph—

A	B
C	D

A – Curbar Edge
B – Sheepwash Bridge, Ashford in the Water
C – Tissington Hall
D – Wirksworth Well-Dressing

ABOUT JOHN N. MERRILL

John combines the characteristics and strength of a mountain climber with the stamina, and athletic capabilities of a marathon runner. In this respect he is unique and has to his credit a whole string of remarkable long walks. He is without question the world's leading marathon walker.

Over the last ten years he has walked more than 55,000 miles and successfully completed ten walks of at least 1,000 miles or more.

His six walks in Britain are—

Hebridean Journey ....1,003 miles
Northern Isles Journey..913 miles
Irish Island Journey ....1,578 miles
Parkland Journey..2,043 miles
Lands End to John O'Groats ....1,608 miles

and in 1978 he became the first person (permanent Guinness Book Of Records entry) to walk the entire coastline of Britain—6,824 miles in ten months.

In Europe he has walked across Austria (712 miles), hiked the Tour of Mont Blanc and GR20 in Corsica as training! In 1982 he walked across Europe—2,806 miles in 107 days—crossing seven countries, the Swiss and French Alps and the complete Pyrennean chain—the hardest and longest mountain walk in Europe.

In America he used the world's longest footpath—The Appalachian Trail (2,200 miles) as a training walk. The following year he walked from Mexico to Canada in record time—118 days for 2,700 miles.

During the summer of 1984, John set off from Virginia Beach on the Atlantic coast, and walked 4,226 miles without a rest day, across the width of America to San Francisco and the Pacific Ocean. This walk is unquestionably his greatest achievement, being, in modern history, the longest, hardest crossing of the USA in the shortest time—under six months (177 days). The direct distance is 2,800 miles.

Between major walks John is out training in his own area —the Peak District National Park. As well as walking in other areas of Britain and in Europe he has been trekking in the Himalayas four times. He lectures extensively and is author of more than sixty books.

CONTENTS

INTRODUCTION

DERBYSHIRE and the Peak District is one of those rare areas which has a complete variety of scenery and historical remains, and the routes in this book embrace almost every village and 'beauty spot' within its boundaries. A map is needed to appreciate fully the attributes of each route, and will greatly enrich one's enjoyment of the area.

The Peakland and South Derbyshire Bonanza routes are primarily introductory, and will help to familiarise the layout of the region before the other runs are undertaken. The majority of these have a set theme, whether it is following in the footsteps of Mary Queen of Scots, just driving over moorland plateaus, or merely connecting one distinctive part of the country to another. There is not sufficient space to extol all the virtues of each run, and instead three or four features are highlighted. It is hoped that these brief notes will encourage you to explore not only from the car seat but also on foot, as one always gets a greater thrill through learning and discovering by looking rather than reading.

Before setting out on a route it is advisable to obtain a copy The Peakland Post, from the Peak Park Planning Board, Aldern House, Bakewell, Derbyshire; or from one of the Tourist Information Offices in the area. It will prove invaluable, not only for its full details of all local functions but also for its lists of the opening times of museums, stately homes and caverns. One of the unique events of Derbyshire is well-dressing, a ceremony being held in some village almost every week during the summer. Village carnivals, sheepdog trials and the opening of private halls and gardens on specific occasions are other factors which will influence the choice of route on a given date.

I have refrained from mentioning 'refreshment' houses, partly because there are so many and also because most people stop when the spirit moves them. I would also emphasise that, although each run is based on a certain town or city, the route can be joined at any point and then followed to complete a circular tour. Finally, I hope that readers will derive as much pleasure as I have done from touring Derbyshire, and will likewise become ardent admirers of this fascinating county.

JOHN N. MERRILL

DERBYSHIRE 1986.

1

Peakland Bonanza—56 Miles

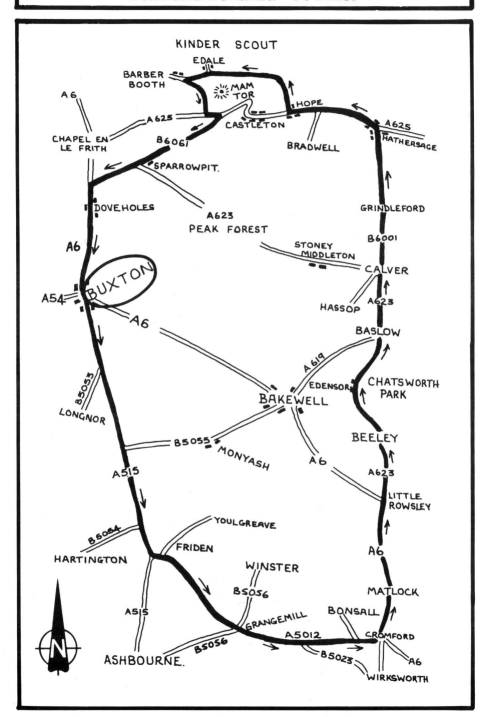

1: PEAKLAND BONANZA

Based on Buxton.

ROUTE: *Buxton—Friden—Grangemill—Cromford—Matlock—Rowsley—Chatsworth—Baslow—Grindleford—Hathersage—Hope—Edale—Mam Tor—Sparrowpit—Dove Holes—Buxton.*

DISTANCE: *56 miles.*

MAPS: *1" O.S. Tourist Edition—'The Peak District'. 1:50,000 O.S.—Sheet No. 119—Buxton, Matlock and Dove Dale. 110—Sheffield and Huddersfield. Bartholomew National Series (1:100,000) No. 29—The Peak and South Yorkshire.*

The basic aim of this route is variety. If you have not visited the area before you can at one fell swoop see the many ingredients which make this perhaps the finest piece of countryside in England. After completing this run through moorland, limestone dales, gritstone edges and past historical houses and villages, you can see what appeals to you for further exploration. It is, as the title suggests, a tremendous route through a tremendous area. Relax and prepare to be astounded by the scenery.

Follow the A515 Ashbourne road from Buxton. The first ten miles to Newhaven and the junction with the A5012 are relatively undramatic. You travel through limestone countryside with lush farming pastures on either side of you, often glimpsing villages and dales. Just before the Newhaven Inn, turn left and follow the A5012 all the way to Cromford. Having passed through the hamlet of Pikehall, you begin the steady descent into Cromford and its delightful surroundings. Past the crossroads at Grangemill, the drive down Griffe Grange Valley is very beautiful. In summer there is an abundance of foliage and dense woodland on both sides and the trees sway in the breeze as you proceed along this gorge of greenery. As you reach Cromford and the B5036, you pass on your left a large village pond where several swans can often by seen.

Turn left onto the B5036 for a few yards, before turning left again onto the A6 and into Matlock Bath. Having passed through woodland, we now come close to the limestone faces. Willersley Castle, built by Sir Richard Arkwright two hundred years ago, is on your right. A little further on, past Arkwright's Mill, more limestone adorns the vale side, and, on reaching Matlock Dale, High Tor comes suddenly into view. It is some 400 feet from the top to the River Derwent below; rock climbers can usually be seen battling against its defences to attain the top. In Matlock Bath there are many places to visit and things to do; the Heights of Abraham reached by cable car, the museums, lovers' walks and boating on the Derwent. Continue on the A6 to Matlock and on through to Darley Dale, with Stanton Moor on your left, towards Rowsley. Instead of turning left into the village, fork right on the B6012 for Beeley, a picturesque gritstone village with a small church which is worth a visit.

Half a mile north of Beeley you meet a set of traffic lights and the bridge over the Derwent. Once across, you are in Chatsworth Park, Derbyshire's most prized possession. As you drive through the unfenced parkland, sheep linger beside the road and, if you are lucky, you may see the herd of fallow deer. Leave your car at one of the car parks and take a stroll in the grounds; and of course a visit to the house and gardens is a must. Leave Chatsworth and continue towards Baslow and on left to Calver; at the traffic lights turn right onto the B6001 for Hathersage. Immediately on your right is another characteristic of the Peak District—a gritstone edge. Curbar and Froggatt Edges, extending to over 70 feet high, are a popular rock climbing ground, and at weekends are festooned with a colourful array of ropes and climbers. At the base of these edges are the villages of Froggatt and Curbar. Fork left in Grindleford and drive along through the woods beside the River Derwent into Hathersage. On nearing the village you will see towering above on your right a man-made gritstone edge called Millstone. The sheer, often overhanging faces reach a height of 120 feet. Hathersage is another of the many charming villages of Derbyshire, and the church here is worthy of a visit. Besides being the resting-place of Little John, Robin Hood's faithful friend, the interior of the church is noble and there are several ancient brasses.

Join the A625 and drive along it for the next four miles to Hope. In doing so you travel much of the length of the Hope Valley. On your left is moorland, while on your right are two small mountains called Win Hill and Lose Hill. Many years ago there was a battle and each hill had an opposing army camped on the top; after the battle the hills were christened according to the fate of the occupiers! At Hope turn right and drive between these two peaks into the Vale of Edale, which forms yet another facet of Derbyshire. On the right is the bleak and extensive moorland plateau of Kinder, while opposite is the mountain chain of Lose Hill, Back Tor and Mam Tor. Edale is a quiet village, nestling against the slopes of Kinder at the southern end of the Pennine Way and excellent walking country. Information on this absorbing area can be obtained from the local Information Office of the Peak Park Planning Board at Fieldhead.

Continue on the lane to Barber Booth, turning left to begin the steep and narrow but short ascent to the pass alongside Mam Tor. A fifteen-minute walk from the nearby carpark leads to the summit, from where there is a wide and enchanting view down the Hope Valley as well as across to Edale and the Kinder plateau. Descend the minor road to the A625, turning left and then right for B6061 and Sparrowpit. If there is time to spare go down the nearby Blue John Cavern, a wonder of Derbyshire and world-renowned for its blue stone and its stalactites and stalagmites.

Pass Eldon Quarry on the left, following the hilly road to the Wanted Inn at Sparrowpit and going straight across to join A623. After just over a mile, a left turn at a 'T' junction leads back to Buxton via the A6 and Dove Holes. I hope this run has created an urge to explore the Peak District in greater depth.

The Crescent, Buxton.

2: PEAT MOORLANDS, PASSES AND RESERVOIRS

Based on Glossop.

ROUTE: *Glossop—Snake Pass—Bamford—Hope—Edale—Chapel-en- le-Frith—Hayfield—Glossop—Woodhead Pass—Langsett—Snake Pass—Glossop.*

DISTANCE: *78 miles.*

MAPS: *1" O.S. Tourist Edition: 'The Peak District'. 1:50,000 O.S. Sheet No. 110—Sheffield and Huddersfield. 1:25,000 O.S. Outdoor Leisure Map—The Dark Peak. Bartholomew National Series (1:100,000) No. 29—The Peak and South Yorkshire.*

This route wanders over the high moorland areas of the northern part of the Peak District National Park. In doing so you enter three counties—Derbyshire, Cheshire and South Yorkshire—and traverse the Snake Pass twice, although in opposite directions. I make no apologies, for the route meanders through exceptionally fine remote countryside and takes in several moorland reservoirs.

Starting from Glossop, a market town situated on the western edge of the peat moors, follow the A57 Sheffield road over the Snake Pass. The highest point on this road is 1,680 feet, from where there is a panoramic view of the aptly named moor of Bleaklow on the left and Featherbed Moss with Kinder Scout beyond on the right. The road descends into open country interspersed with pine forests and passes the Snake Inn, where refreshments can be obtained. Below the Pass is Ladybower Reservoir, which is over two miles long and pleasantly situated among the pine trees. Drive along the left-hand side of the water, turning off before the bridge into Derwent Dale. This slight diversion (a no through road) from the main route is about eleven miles long and leads past Derwent and Howden Reservoirs as well as penetrating deep into Bleaklow. During the summer this road is closed to motor traffic and a bus shuttle service operates up the valley. Cyclists are welcome.

Having crossed the bridge over the reservoir, turn right along A6013 for Bamford. A mile out of Bamford join A625 and turn right for Hope, another pleasant village with a most attractive church, opposite which is the Edale road. Turn right and continue through the Vale of Edale, a beautiful valley bounded on the right by the huge mass of Kinder Scout and on the left by three lesser peaks, Lose Hill, Back Tor and Mam Tor. There is a large car park beside the road junction for Edale village, from where it is only a short walk to the Peak Park Planning Board's Information Office. From the car park turn right to Barber Booth where the road divides, the right-hand fork leading to Upper Booth and the left fork ascending Mam Tor. From the highest point on the Mam Tor road it is possible to climb the summit on foot in a few minutes, and the view from there is well worth the effort. Join A625 and turn right into Chapel-en-le- Frith; at the junction with the Buxton road (A6) turn right and right again onto the A624 for Chapel Milton and Hayfield. This road passes Chinley Churn and again the imposing Kinder plateau, eventually leading to Glossop.

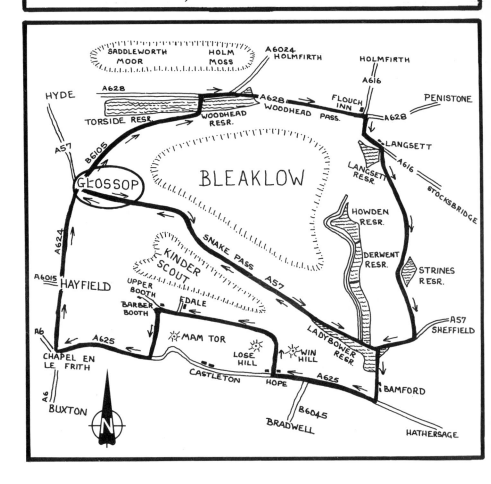

Mam Tor

From the town centre follow B6015 out towards the Woodhead Pass. After a couple of miles there is a good vantage point for viewing the impressive Longdendale with its six reservoirs. Join A628 east of Crowden and turn right towards Sheffield, passing Woodhead Reservoir and climbing the 1,500 feet high Pass. The barren stretch of Langsett Moors is crossed before taking a right turn by the Flouch Inn onto the A616 to Langsett. A little way through the village turn right again over the Langsett Reservoir dam, from where Underbank Reservoir and Stocksbridge can be seen. The road contours the eastern edge of Bleaklow and continues past the Strines Inn, a thirteenth century building, to Strines Reservoir. Two miles past the Inn join the A57, turning right for Glossop and once again passing the Ladybower Reservoir. The ascent of the Snake Pass from this side gives a completely different view; Alport Dale can be seen on the right, and halfway up is Alport Castle, one of the best examples of a landslip in Britain. Two miles beyond the Snake Inn the run is completed by a four-mile descent into Glossop.

Ladybower Inn

The Limestone Dales—63 Miles

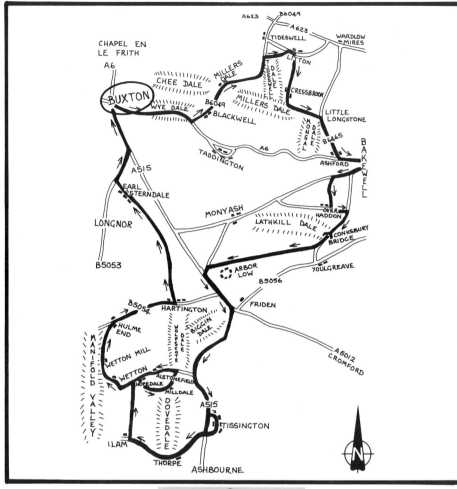

CHAPEL EN LE FRITH

A6

BUXTON

CHEE DALE

MILLERS DALE

WYE DALE

B6049

BLACKWELL

TADDINGTON

A6

A623

B6049

A623

TIDESWELL

WARDLOW MIRES

LITTON

T I D D E A S L W E E L L

MILLERS DALE

CRESSBROOK

LITTLE LONGSTONE

M O N S A L D A L E

B6465

ASHFORD

BAKEWELL

A515

EARL STERNDALE

LONGNOR

B5053

MONYASH

LATHKILL DALE

OVER HADDON

CONKSBURY BRIDGE

YOULGREAVE

ARBOR LOW

B5056

FRIDEN

B5054

HARTINGTON

HULME END

WETTON MILL

WETTON

HOPEDALE

W O L F S C O T E D A L E

BIGGIN DALE

ALSTONEFIELD

MILLDALE

D O V E D A L E

A515

TISSINGTON

A5012 CROMFORD

M A N I F O L D V A L L E Y

ILAM

THORPE

ASHBOURNE

N

Well Dressing

3: THE LIMESTONE DALES

Based on Buxton.

ROUTE: *Buxton—Wye Dale—Blackwell—Litton—Cressbrook— Little Longstone— Bakewell—Over Haddon—Arbor Low—Newhaven—Tissington—Thorpe—Ilam— Dopedale—Milldale—Alstonefield—Wetton Mill—Hulme End—Hartington—Earl Sterndale—Buxton.*

DISTANCE: *63 miles.*

MAPS: *1" O.S. Tourist Edition—'The Peak District'. 1:50,000 O.S. Sheet No. 119—Buxton, Matlock and Dove Dale. Bartholomew National Series (1:100,000)— No. 29—The Peak and South Yorkshire.*

Some of the finest assets of the Peak District are the limestone dales, which are almost incredibly beautiful. They can be fully appreciated from the roadside, although stretching the legs will provide even fuller enjoyment of these fascinating regions. From the Roman spa town of Buxton follow the A6 towards Bakewell, entering the dale country after a few minutes by travelling first through Ashwood Dale and then on to Wye Dale. Limestone buttresses stand out from the valley sides, and the rock is over 2,000 feet thick at Topley Pike; opposite the quarry at this point a track from a car park makes an interesting walk down to Chee Dale and the Monsal Trail.

The road begins to climb, and near the top turn left along B6049 which passes Blackwell village on the left and then meanders through the valley to reach Millers Dale. Take the Tideswell road out of the village, but before climbing the hill turn right along a narrow lane to Litton Mill. This detour leads to the 200 feet high cliff of Raven's Tor, which has a pronounced overhang and forms popular climbing ground. Resume the journey towards Tideswell, after 1½ miles passing Tideswell Dale on your right with a car-park, picnic tables and nature trail. A warden is on duty on most days in the summer, and can direct visitors to the nature trails and other features of interest in this locality.

After another half mile turn right for Litton, and here turn right again for Cressbrook. The lanes are narrow but offer unparalleled views, including a superb prospect of Millers Dale. A steep descent precedes Cressbrook village, where the Little Longstone road involves a climb to Monsal Head and a captivating view down Monsal Dale. Relax and admire the scene by parking the car at the summit car park. From Little Longstone follow B6465 to Ashford and regain the A6 to reach Bakewell, where several cafes provide an opportunity of sampling the famous and truly delicious Bakewell puddings. Climb out of the town on B5055 towards Monyash, and after a mile turn left along a minor road for Over Haddon and the extensive views of Lathkill Dale. If there is time to spare it is worthwhile walking down into this dale from the car park.

Leave the village by the same road as it was entered, but after a few yards turn right past Newclose Farm and then almost immediately right again for Conksbury Bridge and Long Rake. The bridge is not marked on the map, but is the point at which this minor road crosses the River Lathkill, affording an impressive view up Lathkill Dale with Over Haddon in the background. Bear right at all junctions on the road, until after four miles there appears on the left Arbor Low, a stone circle known as the 'Stonehenge of the Peak' and under the guardianship of the Ministry for the Environment. All the 50 stones lie horizontally on the ground, and it is not known whether they were ever upright like Stonehenge.

After half a mile turn left and left again for the A515, and follow the Ashbourne road for nine miles before turning left into Tissington, one of the Derbyshire villages noted for its well-dressing and annually always the first to hold this custom. Each well is dressed with a colourful arrangement of flowers. The 17th Century Hall dominates the village with the Norman Church opposite. The Tissington Trail is nearby, and by leaving your car at the car park you can enjoy a pleasant stroll along a level path.

From Tissington follow the minor road back to the A515 Ashbourne road, cross over and continue towards Thorpe and Ilam. Midway between these two villages, stop at the large car park on the right and leave the car to see Dovedale, the most impressive of all the limestone valleys. At Ilam, noted for its cross, church, hall with National Trust Information Centre and Youth Hostel, which is reputedly haunted, turn right for Stanshope and Hopedale. Here enjoy the extensive views along the side of the Manifold Valley and Dovedale, and then turn right to descend through Sunny Bank to Milldale. This is the northern end of Dovedale; follow the road beside the River Dove for half a mile, and at the 'T'-junction turn left for Alstonefield, continuing straight through the centre of this village and back into Hopedale.

Turn right and then left for Wetton—although now in Staffordshire, it would be wrong not to visit the Manifold Valley on this tour. About a third of a mile from Wetton on the road dropping down to Wetton Mill there is a spectacular view on the left over Thor's Cave, a towering mass of limestone where neolithic remains have been found. Keep to the valley floor and beside the River Manifold to Ecton and Hulme End, where turn right on B5054 for Hartington. This is a particularly fine limestone village complete with its pond and water pump. Take the minor road on the left of the church for Earl Sterndale, 7 miles away; keeping straight ahead at all junctions.

The tall and savage Hitter Hill, Parkhouse Hill and Chrome Hill can be seen on nearing Earl Sterndale, beyond which turn right on to B5053. At the 'T'-junction turn left and follow A515 for the final four miles back into Buxton.

Sheepwash Bridge and River Wye—Ashford in the Water

4: THE GRITSTONE EDGES

Based on Sheffield.

ROUTE: *Sheffield—Owler Bar—Nether End (Baslow)—Bleak House—Curbar—Froggatt—Nether Padley—Fox House Inn—Stanage Edge—Ladybower Reservoir—Rivelin Rocks—Sheffield.*

DISTANCE: *43 miles.*

MAPS: *1" O.S. Tourist Edition 'The Peak District'. 1:50,000 O.S. Sheet No. 110—Sheffield and Huddersfield. 119—Buxton, Matlock and Dove Dale. Bartholomew National Series (1:100,000) No. 29—The Peak and South Yorkshire.*

The Gritstone Edges of Derbyshire form both a rock climbers' haven and a rich as well as striking landscape. They lie along the upper and eastern sections of the valleys, the rock varying in height from 20 to 100 feet. Although in South Yorkshire, Sheffield forms the most logical centre for exploring these outcrops, and this route takes in 16 of them. Leave on the A621 Baslow road, passing through Millhouses, Abbeydale and Totley before the first gritstone moorland—Totley Moor—appears on the right near Owler Bar.

A twisty section over Ramsley Moor precedes a three-mile descent giving views of the gritstone area including Birchens Edge on the left. About 1½ miles from Baslow, the road curves round to the right, and a gritstone crag on the left forms the beginning of the tall and imposing Gardoms Edge rising above the surrounding scenery. Unless wanting to call at one of the several cafes in Baslow, turn left along A619 towards Chesterfield and after a mile pass the escarpment of Chatsworth Edge. Another formation, Birchens Edge, can be seen by turning left at the first road junction and following B6050 for a couple of miles; it can be examined at closer quarters by walking through the stile and along the footpath just past the Robin Hood Inn. On the right of the road is Gibbet Moor, and further ahead a small group of gritstone boulders catches the eye; when viewed from a certain angle, one of them is the exact image of a vulture's head.

After nearly two miles, branch left and almost immediately left again to follow the minor road to Curbar. A further two miles leads to an intersection with the A621, where you should go straight across to Curbar Gap and be rewarded by an expansive view over to Stoney Middleton and Grindleford. On the right is the high and impressive Curbar Edge, offering some of the toughest climbing routes in Derbyshire and thus affectionately called 'Cloggy of the Peak', while on the left is Baslow Edge with its several large buttresses. At the crossroads in Curbar village turn right and follow the minor road into Froggatt, from where it is possible to admire Curbar Edge and also the first part of Froggatt Edge, which has a prominent pinnacle about 50 feet high. The village in fact makes an ideal stopping place, with the Derwent close by, and an excellent walk can be made from the left-hand side of the bridge along the river.

Turn right onto the B6051, and at Grindleford the B6521, to reach the Fox House Inn after about three miles. On the way there are some enthralling views of Froggatt

The Gritstone Edges—43 Miles

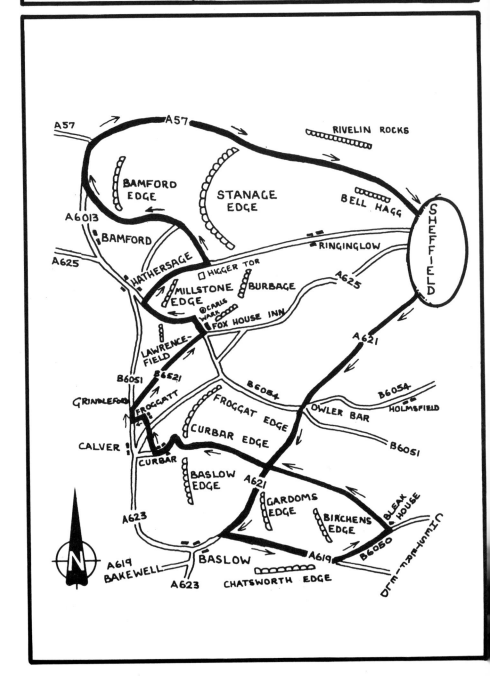

Edge, followed by invigorating glimpses of woodland on the right and moorland interspersed with gritstone outcrops on the left. Near the Inn a majestic building on the right is known as Longshaw Lodge, a National Trust property with cafe, car-park and information centre. Turn left on to A625 for Hathersage, noting several places of interest on the right—Burbage Edge, which can be reached by a stroll up the broad track; the ancient hill fort of Carls Wark erected on a mound of gritstone and 15 minutes' walk from the road; and the unusual rock formation of Toad's Mouth actually alongside the road.

A mile later a sudden right-hand corner reveals the finest vista in the Peak District— the Surprise View up the Hope Valley. It is a remarkable and unforgettable sight when seen for the first time, particularly if it is early morning and the valley is filled with mist, or on a summer's day when shafts of sunlight glisten on the fields and houses.

The black and sombre Millstone Edge stands out on the descent towards Hathersage; after about ¾ mile, turn right along a narrow road which is signposted 'Ringinglow' and almost doubles back on itself. About 1½ miles up this twisting lane a huge leaning block on the right is part of the gritstone outcrop of Higgor Tor, which has some of the hardest routes on gritstone in Derbyshire. Just beyond here the road levels out to provide almost a bird's eye view down on to Burbage Edge. Turn left along another narrow road leading to the vast Stanage Edge. This is some four miles long, and has the almost incredible total of 600 climbs—enough to satisfy the most energetic climber. Turn right at the 'T'junction and follow the road running parallel to the Edge for 3 miles until turning towards Bamford.

Pass Bamford Edge and turn right on meeting A6013 to skirt the eastern side of Ladybower Reservoir. At the A57 turn right for Sheffield and the extremely beautiful final section of the route. The road first runs through a narrow gorge, where gritstone outcrops are intermingled with woodland, passes the beginning of Stanage Edge on the right, and then crosses bleak moorland before dropping down to Rivelin Dams. These are preceded by the solitary Head Stone rising above the moorland on the right, and followed by Rivelin Edge which has a pinnacle about 60 feet high. Bell Hagg, the final gritstone outcrop on this run, can be seen on the right as the road ascends to the Sheffield boundary.

Curbar Edge

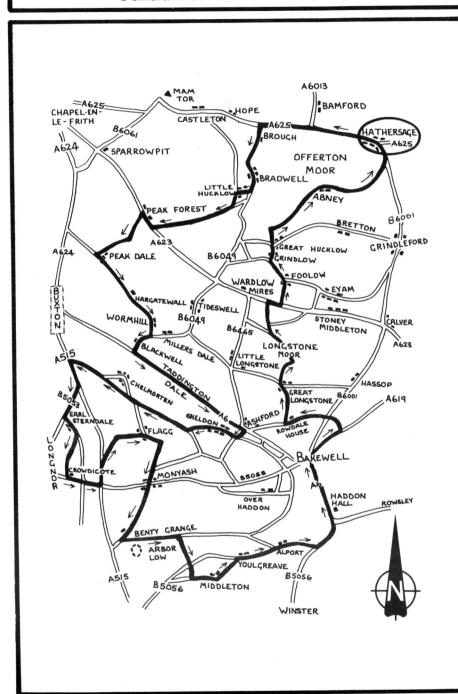

5: CENTRAL PEAKLAND—1

Based on Hathersage.

ROUTE: *Hathersage—Brough—Bradwell—Little Hucklow—Peak Forest—Peak Dale—Wormhill—Millers Dale—Blackwell—Taddington Dale—Ashford—Sheldon— Chelmorton—Earl Sterndale—Middleton—Youlgreave—Alport—Bakewell— Abney— Hathersage.*

DISTANCE: *68 miles.*

MAPS: *1" O.S. Tourist Edition 'The Peak District'. 1:50,000 O.S. Sheet No. 110—Sheffield and Huddersfield. 119—Buxton, Matlock and Dove Dale. Bartholomew National Series (1:100,000) 29—The Peak and South Yorkshire.*

This run provides an opportunity to explore at first hand the beauty and the historic past of the central portion of the Peak District. Hathersage, surrounded by high gritstone moorlands, makes an apt starting point, and of course possesses the grave of Robin Hood's faithful servant—Little John. Leave on A625 heading for Hope, with Offerton Moor forming some particularly attractive scenery on the left. A mile past the High Peak Garden Centre turn left for Bradwell, a former lead mining village in a valley marked by remains of mines and a tall cement work's chimney but otherwise delectable. The road narrows through the village and approaches Hazlebadge Hall with the Vernon coat-of-arms on the wall, while on the left gliders can often be seen floating above Abney Moor. Opposite a lane leading to Great Hucklow, turn right for Little Hucklow, where a barn on the right sports a huge pair of antlers.

Go to the right at the 'T'-junction above the village, and then left to follow the minor road across Tideswell Moor to the A623 where turn right. After a mile the road steeply zigzags and provides an exceptionally fine view of Peak Forest, the one time Gretna Green of the Peak District. The chapel here no longer exists, although much of the stone was used to build the Reading Room; it is possible to learn more about these happenings of yesteryear by visiting the present church dedicated to St. Charles the Martyr. Turn left and bear right for Smalldale, before passing the quarries surrounding the village of Peak Dale with views down to Great Rocks Dale before approaching Wormhill. The church here is one of the 'gems' of the area, and nearby is the James Brindley well and stocks. The 17th Century Wormhill Hall is almost beside the church. Opposite is a signposted path for those who want to take the ten-minute walk to Chee Dale.

On reaching Millers Dale and B6049 turn right towards Blackwell, and then left along the A6 for the enthralling drive down the wooded Taddington Dale and past the entrance of the wide Monsal Dale. Why not stop for a stroll up here? On nearing Ashford turn sharp right and follow a minor road part way up Kirk Dale before again going sharp right, this time into the peaceful and pleasant village of Sheldon. Beyond here turn right and follow the minor road past the outskirts of Chelmorton, turning right on to the A515 at Brierlow Bar and then almost immediately left along B5033. After 1½ miles fork left into the quaint village of Earl Sterndale, where The Quiet Woman public house has a sign depicting a headless lady!

By keeping right at all junctions descend towards Crowdicote, passing the striking pinnacle shape of High Wheeldon and views of staggering proportions over the Longnor peaks of Parkhouse Hill, Chrome Hill and Hollin Hill. The upper reaches of the Dove stretch away in the other direction, while opposite the pinnacle is a limestone climbing ground. Turn sharp left in Crowdicote and head for Monyash; during the climb of the hairpin bends there is an excellent view to the left over the Longnor hills which abruptly erupt above the surroundings. At the A515 turn left and then right for Flagg, where follow minor roads to Monyash. This is an attractive village having a market cross dating back to 1340, as well as an interesting church.

Continue on the minor road through the village to Benty Grange, and just past this house turn left along Long Rake. If Arbor Low, the 'Stonehenge of the Peak', has not been visited, it is on the right and well worth a perusal. After a little over a mile turn right and descend into Middleton, another quiet and 'forgotten' Peak District community, and then continue along B5056 into Youlgreave. The church here is worth visiting, if only to see the alabaster tomb of Sir John Rossington, who holds a heart in his hand. Legend maintains that a hunter caused an act of sacrilege by following his prey into the church, and in penance his heart leapt out!

Descend into Alport and on to the A6, turning left for Bakewell; Haddon Hall is half hidden by trees on the right. Follow A619 out of the town, and in ¾ mile turn left along A6020 before forking right just past Rowdale House. Take the left branch for Great Longstone, and on the perimeter of the village turn right, climbing onto Longstone Moor for views of Bakewell, Bakewell Church and Great Hucklow. At the A623 turn right and then left for Foolow, where bear left past the village green and pond before going right opposite the entrance to Silly Dale. The narrow lane passes through Grindlow, but before entering Great Hucklow turn right, and then after a third of a mile sharp left, up Hucklow Edge towards Abney. The route passes the Derbyshire and Lancashire Gliding Club's airfield, where visitors are encouraged to watch the man-made birds take to the air, and then descend through Abney and past Highlow Hall. There are distant views of Stanage and Millstone Edge before the junction with A622, where turn left for Hathersage.

Haddon Hall

16

6: CENTRAL PEAKLAND—2

Based on Buxton.

ROUTE: *Buxton—Whaley Bridge—Goyt Valley—Goyt's Moss—Axe Edge Moor—Axe Edge—Hollinsclough—Earl Sterndale—Hartington—Biggin—Ashford—Great Longstone—Hassop—Calver—Tideswell—Wheston—Bole Hill—Water Swallows—Buxton.*

DISTANCE: *72 miles.*

MAPS: *1" O.S. Tourist Edition 'The Peak District'. 1:50,000 O.S. Sheet No. 119—Buxton, Matlock and Dove Dale. 110—Sheffield and Huddersfield. 118—The Potteries. Bartholomew National Series (1:100,000) No. 29—The Peak and South Yorkshire.*

Country lanes and good vantage points from which to admire the Peakland landscape are features of this route, and given a fine day any motorist must surely be impressed by the amazing scenery. From Buxton follow A5002 via Long Hill to be rewarded by a glimpse on the left of the Goyt Valley Reservoirs gleaming invitingly. On approaching Whaley Bridge turn left along the B5089 Macclesfield road, and in about a mile again turn left to climb the lane past Wrights Farm to Windgather Rocks—one of the first gritstone climbing grounds to be explored in the area. At a 'T'-junction go left to revel in the sheer beauty of the descent into the Goyt Valley, where bear right alongside the reservoir and enjoy the drive up to Derbyshire Bridge. The captivating fir trees and the expanse of water gradually give way to more barren and wild surroundings. On Sundays the Goyt Valley is closed to traffic but not cyclists. To explore the valley you must leave your car at one of the perimeter car parks and walk.

Just past the bridge turn right and then left to meet the A537; less than two miles away and just outside the Derbyshire boundary is the Cat and Fiddle Inn, one of the highest public houses in the country. Go straight across the main road to the A54, turning left and almost immediately right to cross Axe Edge Moor. Two-thirds of the way over is one of the most impressive views in Derbyshire, with Longnor, its neighbouring hills and the source of the Dove standing out prominently. At the junction with A53 turn right, forking left 1½ miles later and turning abruptly left near the 1,391 ft. triangulation point. The road descends steeply before entering Hollinsclough, a delightful and unspoilt village dominated by the towering masses of Chrome Hill and Parkhouse Hill.

Bear left, following the road below the slopes of Nab End to the B5053, where turn left and cross the River Dove for a particularly exciting run back into Derbyshire as the slopes of Hitter and Parkhouse Hill close in on the road near Glutton. Turn right into Earl Sterndale, bearing left just beyond the church and then right to follow the minor road past High Wheeldon. This is a most memorable drive through limestone country; from Custard Field it is along a shallow valley, but the final section in Long Dale consists of a mixture of grassy slopes and limestone buttresses.

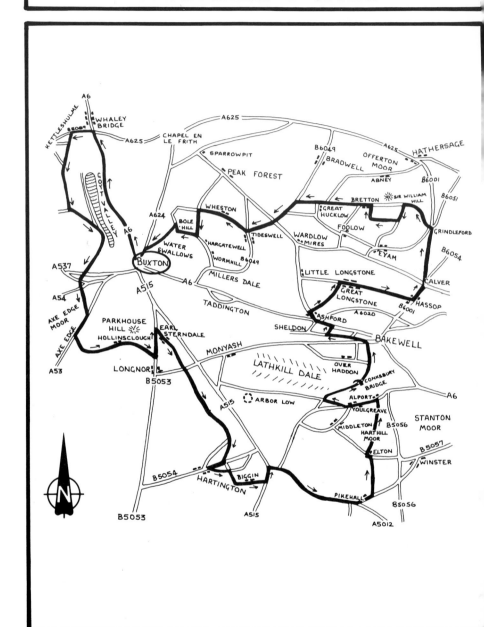

At the junction with B5054 and Hand Dale turn right into Hartington, a charming limestone village which makes an ideal spot to stop and stretch one's legs or partake of some refreshment. Leave by turning right opposite the church to climb the hill past the youth hostel—Hartington Hall—and right again for Biggin. At the far side of this village turn left and follow the A515 road to Newhaven. Here go right along A5012 for Pikehall; a mile past this village bear left on a minor road for Winster, and after a little over a mile turn left at a crossroads for Elton. Opposite the church go left and then right to cross Harthill moor.

This section of the run makes a return to gritstone country, and on the right can be seen the two gritstone towers of Robin Hood's Stride with a stone circle nearby. These interesting formations could perhaps be visited before following the road on its steep descent through a wooded dell and past limestone buttresses to Alport, where turn left to climb B5056 into Youlgreave—another limestone village well worth exploring. Fork right opposite the church for Conksbury Bridge; if time is available, this is another point at which it is worth stopping, not only to admire the view of Lathkill Dale and Over Haddon but also to stroll up the valley beside the river.

At the 'T'-junction turn right towards Bakewell, but unless wanting a Bakewell pudding avoid the town by bearing left past the school and crossing B5055 to take the second road on the right leading down to the A6 and Ashford. Cross the bridge over the River Wye, following B6465 towards Little Longstone and turning right past Thornbridge Hall into picturesque Great Longstone. Here turn right and then left, and after passing the boundary wall of Hassop Hall notice the church on the left with its large bell under the eaves. Proceed to Calver on the B6001, going straight across at the traffic lights and onto Grindleford.

After an extensive tour of the limestone country, it is refreshing to see the gritstone area with its dark stone and rock escarpments along the perimeter of the moorlands, features exemplified by Froggatt and Curbar Edges on the right. In Grindleford keep on the B6001, turning sharp left towards Hathersage, but almost immediately turn left and ascend steeply in the direction of Sir William Hill. The road over the top is unsuitable for cars, so fork left and perhaps pause at Mompesson's Well, one of the furthest points to which occupants of Eyam were allowed to go during the Plague of 1666. This well can be seen below. Turn right just past the well to Highcliffe. Next bear left to traverse the edge of Bretton Moor, going through the desolate and bleak hamlet of Bretton and the Barrel Inn before descending to Great Hucklow.

Follow the minor road to Windmill, turning left on to B6049 for Tideswell—a village of unusual interest, with a church containing many beautiful stained glass windows. Go along the minor road up Brook Bottom for a short distance before turning left to Wheston, where pass the Hall on the left in order to drop down to Dale Head. At the bottom there is a limestone dale on either side, and it is worth stopping to appreciate fully Hay Dale on the right and Peter's Dale—complete with its buttresses—on the left. Turn left at the 'T'-junction, and on the outskirts of Hargatewell fork right to pass the 1,322-ft. Bole Hill on the right. Then fork sharp left to return to Buxton by way of Great Rocks Dale and Water Swallows.

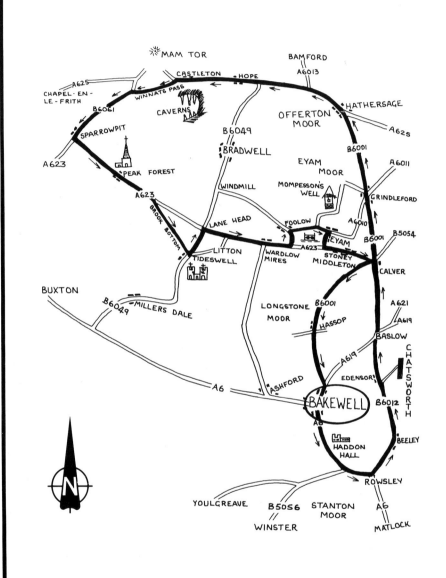

7: HALLS AND CAVERNS

Based on Bakewell.

ROUTE: *Bakewell—Haddon Hall—Rowsley—Beeley—Chatsworth—Baslow—Grindleford—Hathersage—Hope—Castleton—Winnats Pass—Sparrowpit—Peak Forest—Tideswell—Wardlow Mires—Foolow—Eyam—Stoney Middleton—Calver—Hassop—Bakewell.*

DISTANCE: *41 miles.*

MAPS: *1" O.S. Tourist Edition 'The Peak District'. 1:50,000 O.S. Sheet No. 119—Buxton, Matlock and Dove Dale. 110—Sheffield and Huddersfield. Bartholomew National Series (1:100,000) No. 29—The Peak and South Yorkshire.*

PEAKLAND'S showpieces form the theme of this short route, which on a fine summer's day should prove most memorable. Bakewell, is a delightful town full of old houses and alleyways, renowned for the photogenic 14th Century bridge over the River Wye, and the famous delicious Bakewell Puddings. From the roundabout opposite the Rutland Arms Hotel take the A6 Matlock road. Within two miles you reach Haddon Hall, the finest manorial house in England. There is a large car park opposite the entrance to this home of the Manners family, which is open to the public during the summer months on every day of the week except Sundays and Mondays. Here one can see tapestries, the chapel, the banqueting hall and the picturesque gardens, as well as learning of the intriguing love tale of Dorothy Vernon and John Manners, whose tombstones are in the Vernon Chapel of Bakewell Church. Continue to Rowsley, where an old manorial house on the left is now the Peacock Hotel. Turn left along B6012 which by-passes Beeley with its old coaching inn, and two-thirds of a mile later go sharp left to a set of traffic lights and a bridge over the Derwent. This leads to Chatsworth Park with its elusive herd of deer; several well-signposted car parks cater for motorists wishing to stretch their legs in this scenic paradise. Chatsworth House, home of the Dukes of Devonshire and one of the magnificent buildings of Britain, bursts upon the scene without warning as one gains a slight rise. Three hundred years ago Charles Cotton remarked: 'There stands a stately and stupendous pile.'

Keep along the B6012, passing the model village of Edensor with its attractive houses and church where many of the Dukes of Devonshire lie buried. There is an excellent cafe in some old stables beside the post office. The next 15 miles consists of a pleasant run along the Hope Valley and past many interesting settlements; at Baslow one of the clocks on the church tower has the words 'Victoria 1897' instead of numbers, and inside there is a dog whip used in the 17th Century to whip the dogs out of the church before the service began. Turn left along the A623 to the traffic lights at Calver Slough. Turn right along B6001, passing the gritstone edge of Froggatt on the right and turning left at Grindleford for Hathersage. An alternative, if time is available, is to go along B6001 for a mile and then turn off for Upper Padley to walk for about a third of a mile along the track to the historic Padley Chapel. The fascinating interior has stained-glass windows depicting the Padley Martyre who were brutally hanged in Derby in 1588.

Turn left in Hathersage onto the A625 for Hope and Castleton. At Castleton the first feature to arrest your attention is Peveril Castle, towering above the village and reached by a steep walk up to the 12th century battlements. Down at ground level the Douglas Museum contains some unique specimens of painstaking work—one example is the Lord's Prayer, written by hand on a piece of paper which will pass through the eye of a small needle! But Castleton's main claim to fame is its four caverns full of stalactites and Blue John stone. Peak Cavern, reached by walking up a narrow cleft from the village, has an impressive entrance. Speedwell Cavern is approached by continuing on the A625 towards Winnats Pass, and is memorable for the fact that part of the subterranean journey is by boat. Treak Cliff Cavern has some notable formations, while the last cavern is Blue John underneath Mam Tor.

Ascend Winnats Pass and turn left along B6061 for Sparrowpit, where turn left on A623 for Peak Forest—many years ago the centre of the royal forest, and between 1728 and 1754 the 'Gretna Green of England'. After 2½ miles turn right along Brook Bottom into Tideswell, an interesting village where the church is known as 'the Cathedral of the Peak' and contains some exceptionally fine stained-glass. Turn left and rejoin the A623 at Lane Head (Anchor Inn) and turn right. A mile past Wardlow Mires turn left for Foolow, where turn right for Eyam—Derbyshire's most famous village. It was struck by the Plague in 1665-6, and reminders of this tragedy are plaques on the cottages, gravestones in the churchyard and mementos to the Rev. Mompesson, the then Rector who gave unyielding help to the local people. Eyam Hall, the village stocks, a bull ring and a Saxon cross are further features to visit. Turn right and join the A623 near Stoney Middleton for the awe-inspiring drive past the limestone buttresses of Middleton Dale, and at Calver Slough turn right to follow the B6001 through Hassop and back to Bakewell.

Chatsworth House

8: UNUSUAL ROCKS

Based on Matlock.

ROUTE: *Matlock—Rowsley—Stanton-in-Peak—Birchover—Cratcliffe Tor—Winster—Grangemill—Longcliffe—Brassington—Black Rocks—Longcliffe—Wirksworth Moor—Alport Hill—Whatstandwell—Crich—Holloway—Lea—Riber—Tansley—Matlock—Bonsall—Cromford—Matlock.*

DISTANCE: *47 miles.*

MAPS: *1" O.S. Tourist Edition 'The Peak District'. 1:50,000 O.S. Sheet No. 119—Buxton, Matlock and Dove Dale. Bartholomew National Series (1:100,000)—No. 29—The Peak and South Yorkshire. No. 24—Derby and Nottingham.*

THE THEME of this route is rocks of unusual type and structure, features of interest not only in themselves but also for the magnificent views obtained from them of places ranging from a zoo to a rhododendron garden. Leave Matlock on the A6 for Rowsley, and opposite the Peacock Hotel turn sharp left to climb the minor road to Stanton-in-Peak, where the church has several interesting wood carvings. Stanton Moor can be driven round in two ways, both of which have much to offer, but an even better scheme is to park the car and spend a pleasant half hour visiting the ancient monuments of King's Stone, Nine Ladies Stone Circle and Earl Grey Tower.

Descend into Birchover by passing several quarries, world renowned for the unique Stanton Stone which has been used in the construction of such majestic buildings as Sheffield Cathedral. The road abruptly turns right opposite the Druid Inn, behind which the small hill of Rowtor Rocks contains passageways, tunnels, stairways, armchairs, and a couple of rocking stones, all reputedly the work of the Druids but in fact made in the 18th Century. Descend to the B5056, turning left, and within half a mile come to some more interesting rock formations on the right, reached by a track from the roadside. The high gritstone crag of Cratcliffe Tor has at the left of its base the shallow Hermit's Cave, protected by a wrought-iron grid through which can be seen niches and a crucifix carved into the rock. To the left is Robin Hood's Stride, another gritstone outcrop with two tall towers, which were once known as Mock Beggars Hall and which have at their back a stone circle.

After about half a mile turn sharp left at a crossroads to visit the interesting limestone village of Winster, where the old Market Hall—now owned by the National Trust—is of particular note. Turn right up West Bank to rejoin B5056 and turn left for Grangemill. Go straight across A5012 to pass through a thick wood, which in summer forms an invigorating drive underneath a tunnel of green foliage. At the crossroads at Longcliffe turn left for the typical Derbyshire limestone village of Brassington, where go right and right again to climb a short hill. At the top the car can be parked and a walk taken through a field to the delightful picnic spot of Rainster Rocks, notable for being one of the few examples in Britain of a dolomitic formation.

Continue on to the B5056, turning right, and after half a mile passing on the left Pinder's Rock, a limestone outcrop with ivy-clad tower. At Longcliffe turn right, and at the next road left, to see Harborough Rocks, which with the formations at Rainster form a collective

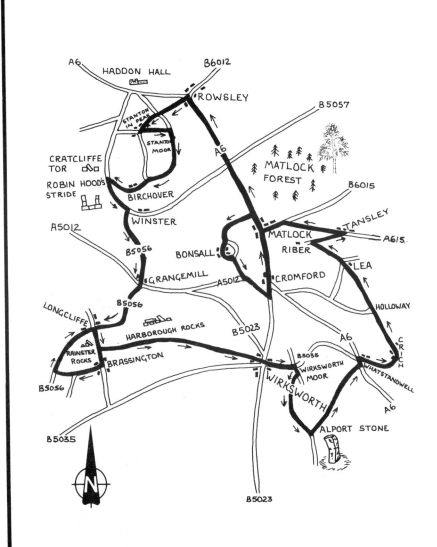

group known as Brassington Rocks. The road reaches the mining village of Wirksworth, where the church to St. Mary the Virgin contains the Wirksworth Stone and monuments to the Gell family. Sir John Gell was Parliamentary Governor of Derbyshire at the time of the Civil War.

Follow B5035 to Wirksworth Moor, bearing right and then turning sharp right along a minor road through Gorsey Bank to Alport Hill. This small piece of land owned by the National Trust has a car park within yards of the summit, where there is a tall gritstone boulder and an almost unbelievably extensive view. Turn left and go past the imposing Alderwasley Hall, 3 miles away, now a school, and on meeting the A6 turn right and cross the River Derwent to bear left for Whatstandwell and Crich. Here the Tramway Museum contains working trams from many parts of Britain—including Sheffield's last tram—as well as from places such as Czechoslovakia. The nearby monument to the Sherwood Foresters is admirably sited, and the light from the beacon can be seen from six counties.

Continue to Holloway and the outskirts of Lea, where the Rhododendron Gardens are open to the public during the early part of the summer. Follow the minor road to Riber, with its old Hall and the useful landmark of Riber Castle. This has been gutted by fire, but together with the grounds and outbuildings now houses an extensive collection of Britain's wildlife, and a pleasant hour can easily be spent here. Turn right, and at Tansley turn left along A615 for Matlock, but the run has not yet finished. Indeed, a climax is formed by crossing the A6 bridge and turning right towards Snitterton before taking the first left along the narrow Salter Lane.

The adventurous drive is rewarded by extensive views down Darley Dale on the right before coming to a 'T'-junction, where turn left for Bonsall. On the left-hand side of a sharp right-hand corner is a market cross with thirteen circular steps tapering to a solitary pillar. Head towards Cromford, passing on the left a large pond with an old waterwheel, and at the next two 'T'-junctions turn left so as to join the A6. On the right, surrounded by trees, is Willersley Castle, once the home of Sir Richard Arkwright whose cotton mill is a little further up the road and can be visited, with the Cromford Canal opposite. Turn left onto the A6 and entering Matlock from the Cromford direction forms a fitting end to the 'unusual rocks' tour, for high on the right is a sheer limestone face which increases in grandeur until the huge bastion of High Tor commands attention.

Alport Stone

Jeffcoats Pinnacle

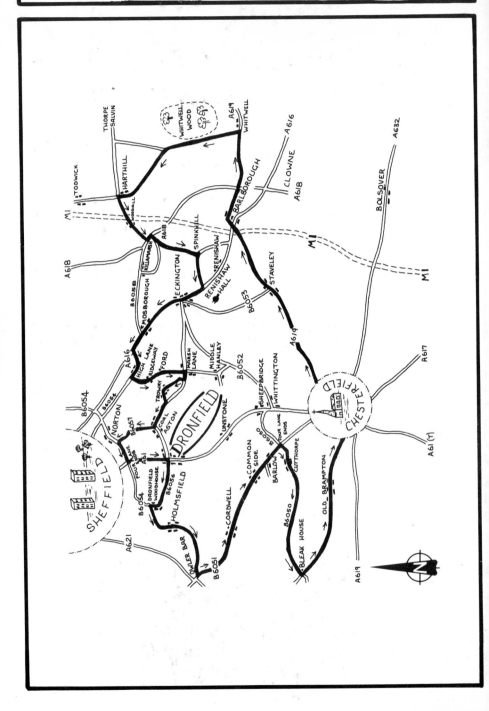

9: 'TRANSFORMATION'

Based on Dronfield.

ROUTE: *Dronfield—Holmsfield—Owler Bar—Cordwell Valley—Barlow—Four Lane Ends—Cutthorpe—Bleak House—Old Brampton—Chesterfield—Staveley—Barlborough—Whitwell—Harthill—Killamarsh—Spinkhill—Renishaw—Eckington—Mosborough—Highlane—Marsh Lane—Troway—Coal Aston—Norton—Dronfield.*

DISTANCE: *53 miles.*

MAPS: *1:50,000 O.S. Sheet Nos.—110 Sheffield and Huddersfield. 120 Mansfield and the Dukeries. 119 Buxton, Matlock and Dove Dale. Bartholomew National Series (1:100,000)—No. 29—The Peak and South Yorkshire.*

ALTHOUGH this route goes close to the two major industrial areas of Sheffield and Chesterfield, it still has many surprises in the form of unspoilt villages with their ancient churches and old halls. Dronfield is a rapidly expanding satellite town of Sheffield, although the area around the High Street with its 16th Century Blue Stoops coaching inn and church to St. John the Baptist retains much 'village' atmosphere. The church has many pieces of historic value, such as a 900 year old preaching cross, a Tudor pulpit, the Fanshawe brasses and, the finest assets of all, the chancel and the huge eastern window. Follow B6056 through Stubley and Dronfield Woodhouse, and at the junction with B6054 turn left for Holmsfield, where the parish church of St. Swithin has a fascinating interior complete with a gallery. There are extensive views over the skyscraper city of Sheffield on the way to Owler Bar.

Opposite the Peacock Inn descend B6051, driving for the next three miles down the Cordwell Valley, which during May and June is a riot of colour with both sides a mass of rhododendron flowers. The dream setting ends at the approach to Commonside; another mile leads to the quaint hamlet of Barlow, and a further mile to Four Lane Ends (Upper Newbold), where turn right along B6050. Pass through Cutthorpe and Ingmanthorpe, and on the ascent of Grange Hill notice the expansive view behind over Chesterfield. There are several old stone signposts on the right near Bleak House, where turn left for a delightful drive with glimpses of Chesterfield and its crooked spire before reaching Old Brampton. Here a beautiful parish church has two stone figures on the outside of the south wall representing its patron saints, Peter and Paul.

Red House (on left) Dronfield

Chesterfield is a pleasing town combining the old with the new. The shopping area has been revitalised and is most attractive. The Peacock Inn is now a Heritage and Information Centre. Follow the A619 to Staveley, entering the world of industry for a brief period before returning to the county at Barlborough. The church here is worth visiting, as are the Van Dyke Nurseries a mile hence. In another 1½ miles turn left and follow the country lane into Harthill. Turn left for Woodhall and at the A618 go left and then right, to ascend a short hill which has the tall and imposing cluster of buildings of Mount St. Mary's Roman Catholic College on its right. Turn right in Spinkhill, descending into Renishaw; shortly after turning right on to A616, Renishaw Park can be seen on the left and, between the foliage, glimpses of the impressive Renishaw Hall. Traverse the outskirts of Eckington to enter Mosborough, and a mile north of this village turn left along B6054 into Highlane, here going left for the descent to Ford via Ridgeway and Ridgeway Moor. There are several small reservoirs on the right on the climb to Marsh Lane, where turn right and almost immediately right again. From the first part of this road there is a panoramic view ahead of Sheffield.

A farm track opposite a left-hand bend in Troway leads past Fold Farm Cottage; a short walk down here brings one to some delightful woodland and reservoirs. Continue along the road, turning right for Coal Aston, and here going right for Norton-in-Sheffield but on the boundary of Derbyshire, with which it has many ties. Sir Francis Chantery, a very capable and talented sculptor, was born in Norton and has a plaque in the splendidly located church. Descend to Four Lane Ends, turning left (A61) to return to the centre of Dronfield in another two miles.

Crooked Spire, Chesterfield

10: A MIXED BAG

Based on Chesterfield.

ROUTE: *Chesterfield—Barlow—Bolehill—Crowhole Reservoir—Ramsley Reservoir—Clod Hall—Beeley—Rowsley—Gladwin's Mark—Northedge—Alton—Old Tupton—North Wingfield—Heath—Sutton Scarsdale—Arkwright Town—Staveley—Eckington—Whittington—Chesterfield.*

DISTANCE: *55 miles.*

MAPS: *1:50,000 O.S. Sheet Nos. 119—Buxton, Matlock and Dove Dale. 120—Mansfield and the Dukeries. Bartholomew National Series (1:100,000)— No. 29—The Peak and South Yorkshire.*

THE first half of the route wanders to and fro exploring the many picturesque hamlets and bleak moorlands on the fringe of the National Park, while the second part takes in further villages among the mining areas around Chesterfield. Some of the lanes followed are narrow, but this should merely add to the pleasure for it means one is getting to grips with the region and learning its hidden secrets. From Chesterfield follow B6051 through Newbold and Four Lane Ends (Upper Newbold) to the 'olde worlde' hamlet of Barlow. Opposite the circular railing protecting an oak tree stump, turn left towards Bolehill; the house near the summit is worth a second look, for it is indeed old and the ivy cladding gives an air of mystery. Descend the hill and turn right for Wilday Green. A steep climb follows, and on the left Crowhole Reservoir can be seen before forking left at the minor road and passing through Moorhall. Turn left at a junction, and very shortly on the right is another expanse of water, Ramsley Reservoir.

At the A621 turn left and then left again, ascending slightly with moorland either side past Clod Hall to the junction at Bleak House. Part way along on the right can be seen the pinnacle of Nelson's Monument on Birchens Edge. Go straight on at the crossroads, heading for Old Brampton, and at the next crossroads bear right to pass the delightfully named Puddingpie Hill on the left. Cross A619 and continue round the edge of Brampton East Moor past Loads Head, bearing right at all junctions to enjoy a memorable view over Lindup Woods before reaching Beeley. This is a fascinating village, full of old houses, the Devonshire Arms being a former coaching inn. The church is of interest, if only because of the basson hanging inside; it was used to accompany the hymns until 1750, when an organ was fitted. Turn left onto the B6012, passing a large millstone indicating a brief entry into the National Park. Just before the A6 road in Rowsley go sharp left and climb the 1 in 5 gradient back onto Beeley Moor, turning right at the crossroads before Gladwin's Mark. Go straight on at all subsequent crossroads, driving beside Matlock Forest on the right until bearing left just past the 1,044 ft. triangulation point at Wire Stone. Turn left, the narrow lane passes many old buildings, which otherwise would be missed, until it comes to Uppertown, where go straight on to Stone Edge.

Turn right onto the B5057, heading for Walton and on the left passing some exciting moorland where a house has been built underneath a large overhang of rock; on your right is the Red Lion Inn. Bear left at the junction with A632, and soon afterwards turn right past Harpur Hill House and onto the outskirts of Wingerworth. Keep right at the junction

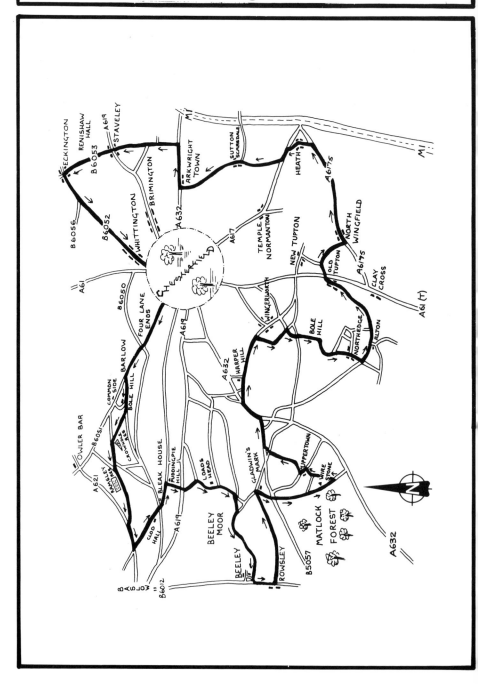

on the village boundary, and on reaching the crossroads turn right to go over another crossroads before forking left and climbing to the 770-ft. summit of Bole Hill. More country lanes lead down to Northedge and curve round to the hamlet of Alton; from here descend to the minor road near Woodthorpe Mill before bearing left and driving past Woodthorpe Hall into Old Tupton. At the roundabout with A61 go straight across and down Hepthorne Lane to North Wingfield. The diversion is to visit the parish church of St. Lawrence, which has a magnificent rood arch, and above it, to the right, part of a painting detailing the ten commandments and dating back to the 16th Century. Turn left onto the A6175 and drive through Holmewood until near the M1, when turn left for Heath and the A617. Here bear left, and soon afterwards turn right and cross the A617.

Near Sutton Scarsdale is an impressive ruined Hall on the right; if time is available, visit the interesting church alongside this once majestic building. Continue into Arkwright Town, turning right at the junction with A632 and a mile later turning left to reach the A619 and the centre of Staveley. Before leaving this industrial town have a look at the church, which has several tombs of the Frenchville family and one stained window portraying their coat of arms. From Staveley follow B6053, passing the entrance to Renishaw Hall, built by the Sitwell family who founded an iron works at nearby Eckington. Follow B6056 out of Eckington before turning left along B6052 to reach Old Whittington. On the right is the thatched Revolution House, in which three men—the Earl of Devonshire, the Earl of Danby and John D'Arcy—met in 1688 and made plans that led to the dethronement of James 11 and the accession of William 111. Continue on to Whittington Moor and Chesterfield.

Thorpe Salvin Church Font

Town and Country—54 Miles

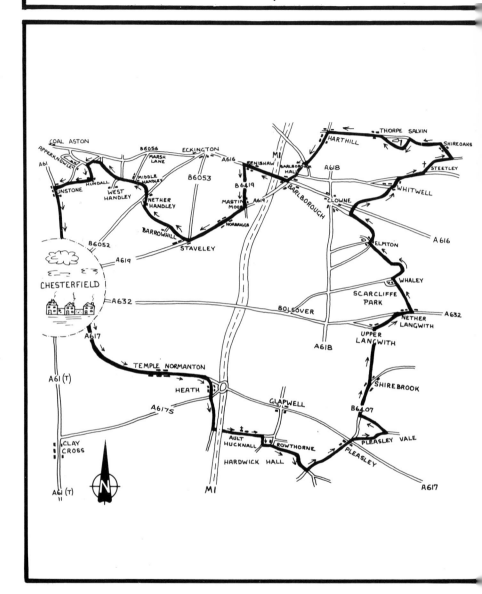

Join A616 for Renishaw, and in the village turn left along B6419 to Mastin Moor. At the junction with A619 turn right into Norbriggs and Staveley. Follow the signs for Handley to turn right, and pass Staveley Chemical Works on the left. Beyond Nether Handley cross B6052 into Middle Handley, bearing left to follow a country lane towards Apperknowle. Before entering this quiet village turn left for the hamlet of Hundall—towering above the houses at prominent height is a tall T.V. mast. Descend to Unstone and the A61, turning left and returning to Chesterfield.

11: TOWN AND COUNTRY

Based on Chesterfield.

ROUTE: *Chesterfield—Temple Normanton—Heath—Pleasley Vale—Upper Langwith—Whaley—Elmton—Clowne—Whitewell—Steetley—Shireoaks—Thorpe Salvin—Harthill—Barlborough—Renishaw—Mastin Moor—Norbriggs— Apperknowle—Hundall—Unstone—Chesterfield.*

DISTANCE: *54 miles.*

MAPS: *1:50,000 O.S. Sheet No. 110—Sheffield and Huddersfield. 119—Buxton, Matlock and Dove Dale. 120—Mansfield and the Dukeries. Bartholomew National Series (1:100,000)—No. 29—The Peak and South Yorkshire.*

THIS route is close to the industrial areas and often encroaches into their domain, but nevertheless it takes in several hidden and forgotten delights of Derbyshire. Leave Chesterfield on the A617 Mansfield road, going through mining and agricultural land. At Temple Normanton turn right for Heath. One moment it is a modern environment and the next a stone-built farming community—it's a delightful transition! Cross A6175, noticing the tall towers of Hardwick Hall ahead, and instead of going into Stainsby turn left under the M1 and into the Hamlet of Ault Hucknall. Beside Hucknall Farm is the church of St. John the Baptist, which has a couple of arches in the chancel dividing it into two little rooms. One portion contains the choir stalls and the other the altar, and from the back of the church they are pleasingly reminiscent of monastic architecture. The other item of interest is a large tomb with five alabaster figures on the edge of the lid; it is to Anne Kighley, wife of the first Earl of Devonshire, who died in 1628.

Continue along the lane to Rowthorne and down to Newboundmill Farm, turning left here into Pleasley and crossing the A617 to follow the B6407 for ¼ mile before branching right down Pleasley Vale. Turn left, and in half a mile rejoin the B6407 and turn right for Shirebrooks, continuing straight ahead at the crossroads on the village outskirts for Upper Langwith. At the 'T'-junction fork right, and in due course merge with the A632 before turning sharp left in Nether Langwith to pass some small lakes and Scarcliffe Park on the left. Continue past the red- tiled roofs of Elmton, but instead of going into Clowne turn right to meet the A616 where again go right. Follow this road for a mile before forking left into the village of Whitewell.

From here ascend the B6043 to the A619, turning right, and a little over a mile later bearing left, to reach Steetley church. Derbyshire has many usual buildings, but it would be hard to find anywhere a small church of such magnificence. It measures 52 feet long by 15 feet wide, and is one of those gems which one admires and never forgets. Continue along the lane to the junction at Holme Carr, where turn left, making a brief entry into Nottinghamshire. Cross the ford into Shireoaks, turning left and left again at Netherthorpe. On rounding the corner several Cessna aircraft are visible; this is the home of the Sheffield Aero Club, and it makes a delightful change to watch these plans take off and land with effortless ease. At Thorpe Salvin keep left for Harthill, where turn left past the church to drive along a street which was the 'Harthill Walk' of Scott's Ivanhoe. Turn right and immediately left at Nitticarhill, and follow the minor road to Barlborough, passing on the right the impressive building of Barlborough Hall.

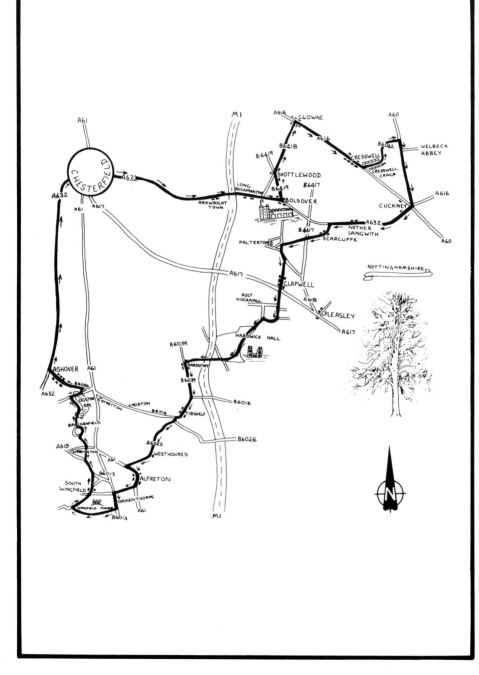

12: TWO LADIES

Based on Chesterfield.

ROUTE: *Chesterfield—Bolsover—Creswell—Welbeck Abbey—Cuckney—Nether Langwith—Scarcliffe—Palterton— Glapwell—Hardwick Hall—Hardstoft—Tibshelf—Westhouses—Alfreton—Oakenthorpe—Wingfield Manor—South Wingfield—Wessington—Ogston Reservoir—Ashover—Chesterfield.*

DISTANCE: *59 miles.*

MAPS: *1:50,000 O.S. Sheet Nos. 119—Buxton, Matlock and Dove Dale. 120—Mansfield and the Dukeries. Bartholomew National Series (1:100,000) No. 29— The Peak and South Yorkshire. No. 24—Derby and Nottingham.*

Bess of Hardwick and Mary Queen of Scots both have a permanent place in the history of Derbyshire. Bess, the wife of George the sixth Earl of Shrewsbury, who was guardian of Mary, has left us with a colourful life story and several impressive buildings. The Scottish Queen was held captive in several of the Earl's Derbyshire residences, carving a sad tale in English royal history. Places associated with these two historical figures are visited on this run, which leaves Chesterfield via the A632 to pass through Long Duckmanton before giving views of the impressively situated Bolsover Castle. This is cared for by the Ministry for the Environment and is largely in ruins except for the Little Castle with its 'chateau' like lines.

Turn left along B6419, and at the crossroads in Shuttlewood go right on B6418 for Clowne. At the 'T'-junction with A616 turn right for Creswell, a mining village near the Derbyshire boundary and close to the renowned Creswell Crags, now a country park—perhaps a stroll here? Here many relics of early man have been unearthed, and the numerous caverns include Robin Hood's Cave. Turn left and follow B6042 past the crags until it meets the A60 from Worksop; here turn right to enter Nottinghamshire for a brief period. On the left is Welbeck Abbey, part of which is a college and market garden. At Cuckney turn right for the A632, going through the village of Nether Langwith, and then two miles from the centre of Bolsover branching left to cross the B6417 on the outskirts of Scarcliffe. At the 'T'-junction before Palterton fork left, and after just over half a mile turn right and continue into Glapwell, where signposts indicate the way to Rowthorne and Hardwick Hall.

The Hall was owned by the Cavendish family (the Dukes of Devonshire) until 1959; it was the home of Bess the Countess of Shrewsbury, and is now under the guardianship of the National Trust. The old Hall where Bess was born still stands nearby, and on top of all the towers are the tall initials E.S., standing for Elizabeth Shrewsbury. Drive right through the grounds, and just past the Hardwick Inn take the second left for Hardstoft, on the other side of this village meeting the B6039, where turn left and continue to Alfreton via Tibshelf and Westhouses (B6025). Take the A615 Matlock road, and after two miles fork left at Fourlane Ends crossroads to encircle Wingfield Manor.

On the right beyond Oakenthorpe can be seen Wingfield Manor, a ruin of historical importance, reached by taking the second road on the right and branching right after 1½ miles on joining B5035. Leave the car at the gates to the Manor and walk up the rough

Bolsover Castle

track to the ruin, owned by the Earls of Shrewsbury and having a crypt and a 70ft. high tower. Mary Queen of Scots spent many months here. Continue to South Wingfield on the B5035 and turn left and almost immediately turn left again onto a lane for Wessington and A615. Turn left at the A615 and on a sharp left-hand corner, just before entering Wessington, go straight across along the minor road and at the 'T'-junction fork right and shortly afterwards left to take the right-hand road round the village of Brackenfield. Turn right beside the church to follow a road meandering beside the ornithologist's favourite haunt of Ogston Reservoir.

At the other side of Woolley turn right along B6014 and soon afterwards left to merge with B6036. Two miles away is Ashover, notable for the interesting church which has several tombs of the Babington family. Anthony Babington tried to organise a rescue attempt to remove Mary Queen of Scots from Wingfield, but was discovered and executed shortly before Mary. Continue along B6036, forking right on meeting A632, and in just over six miles reaching the centre of Chesterfield. If it was missed at the outset, the parish church with its crooked spire has an impressive interior and is 'a must'.

Hardwick Hall

13: SOUTH DERBYSHIRE BONANZA

Based on Derby.

ROUTE: *Derby—Mackworth—Brailsford—Ashbourne—Clifton—Sudbury—Hatton— Hilton—Willington—Swarkestone—Chellaston—Elvaston—Borrowash—Risley—Dale— West Hallam Common—Morley—Derby.*

DISTANCE: *61 miles.*

MAPS: *1:50,000 O.S. Sheet Nos. 128—Derby and Burton-upon-Trent. 129—Nottingham and Loughborough. Bartholomew National Series (1:100,000)— No. 24—Derby and Nottingham.*

THE part of Derbyshire south of the Peak District National Park is equally as beautiful as its northern counterpart. It may not have such a diverse range of exciting scenery, but it is a peaceful area full of country hamlets and some unique historical remains. This route provides a good introduction to the region; leave Derby by the A52, and on the perimeter of the city boundary turn right down the lane which ambles through the village of Mackworth. Take a close look at the church and the remains of a castle before rejoining the A52 and passing Kirk Langley and Brailsford to reach the attractive town of Ashbourne. If time permits, a walk round and a visit to St. Oswald's church should prove enjoyable.

Take the A515 through Clifton, one of the assets of this nine-mile stretch being that almost every mile or so there is a minor village. So if a name appeals or a place looks attractive, simply turn off and explore its secrets. Just beyond Sudbury Prison, turn left and follow the A50 for the next four miles; on your right is the handsome village of Sudbury, with the National Trust-owned Sudbury Hall. This stretch is close to the River Dove and the county boundary, and again there are roads on either side leading into the quiet corners of the area. The battlements of the admirably placed fortification of Tutbury, just in Staffordshire but having close ties with many historical happenings in Derbyshire, can be seen on your right from Hatton. Here leave A50 by going straight along A516 to Hilton, where turn right onto the A5132 and cross the A38 and the Trent and Mersey Canal into Willington. For a digression turn right further along the A5132 and visit the cluster of dwellings by the River Trent at Twyford before passing through Barrow upon Trent and seeing the long and historic bridge at Swarkestone.

Sudbury Hall

37

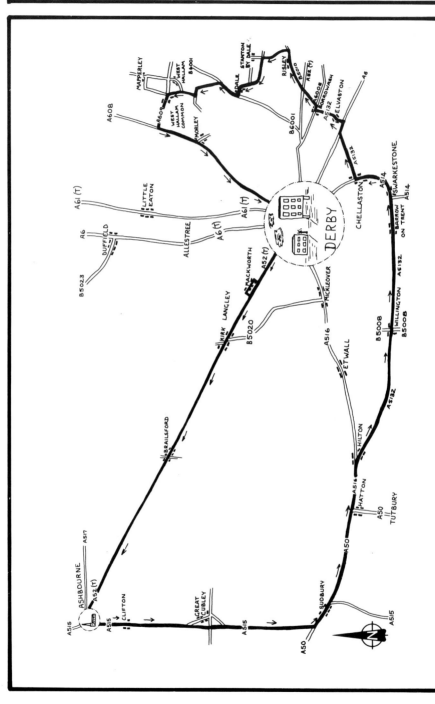

Green Man Sign—Ashbourne

Keep straight on here, and follow the A514 for the next mile to Chellaston, where turn right along A5132 then B5010 for Elvaston and Borrowash. Keep to the B5010 to Risley. Half a mile from the church turn left onto the country lane towards Stanton by Dale, but before the village bear left at a crossroads for Dale—a place where one parks the car, wanders around the historical remains, and never forgets what has been seen. Standing in a field is a tall archway, all that survives of the Abbey except for a nearby house which has been built from some of the ruins. The church here is also unusual, for it is combined with a farmhouse, and closeby is a hermit's cave.

Just north of Dale turn right onto A6096, and half a mile later turn left past the windmill, keeping to the outskirts of West Hallam so as to fork left at Stanley Common onto the A609. Two miles later, at the junction with A608, bear left for Derby, and after a further two miles turn left and descend to the church to St. Matthew at Morley. Inside are four large windows, which originally came from Dale Abbey and now form the most spectacular range of stained glass in the country. Rejoin the A608 and return to Derby.

Elvaston Castle

Along the Lanes—57 Miles

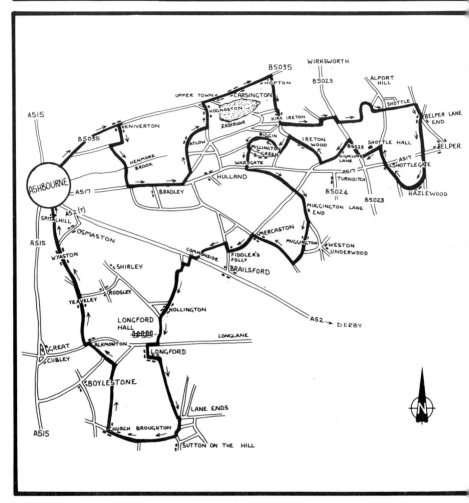

forking left and climbing gradually to the delightfully named house of Fiddlers Folly. Turn right, and at the next junction left, for Commonside, where go to the right along A52 for a few yards before turning left for Hollington. On the way the majestic Ednaston Hall can be seen on the right. Continue past Longford Hall, also on the right, and into Longford where cross Sutton Brook to follow Longford Lane as far as Lane Ends and Sutton on the Hill. Turn right and cross the brook a second time to enter Church Broughton, turning right just west of the village to follow the lane past Alkmonton Hall, the hamlet of Alkmonton and into Yeaveley. Continue into Wyaston, and just north of here bear left past Osmaston Pastures before descending steeply into Ashbourne.

I have refrained from giving details of churches and other items of interest on this route for there are so many that it is perhaps best to choose as one drives along. It is a run where the absence of details enables the motorist to enjoy discovering many hidden secrets.

14: ALONG THE LANES

Based on Ashbourne.

ROUTE: *Ashbourne—Kniveton—Henmore Brook—AtlowHognaston—Upper Town—Kirk Ireton—Shottlegate—Shottle Hall—Highcliffe Lane—Wardgate—Mugginton Lane End—Muggington—Mercaston—Fiddlers Folly—Commonside—Hollington—Longford—Lane Ends—Ashbourne.*

DISTANCE: *57 miles.*

MAPS: *1:50,000 O.S. Sheet Nos. 119—Buxton, Matlock and Dove Dale. 128—Derby and Burton-upon-Trent. Bartholomew National Map Series (1:100,000)—No. 24— Derby and Nottingham.*

This route goes through the very heart of the countryside along narrow lanes and has an air of adventure, so fasten the seat belts, drive slowly and admire to the full the scenery and delightful hamlets passed on the way. Time is of no importance, for one enters a peaceful world of quaint cottages, churches commanding the centre points of the villages, impressive Halls surrounded by extensive gardens, and farms amid picturesque settings.

From Ashbourne follow the B5035 Wirksworth road for three miles to Kniveton, a pleasant and quiet village crystallising what is in store. Turn right and follow the hilly lane down Kniveton Brook, and on the summit of a short rise fork sharp left to descend to Henmore Brook and the A517. Turn left, and just over a mile later bear left again for Atlow, an invigorating drive through farmland which on a still summer's day cannot be equalled. Continue along the lane, climbing to Turlow Fields before dropping down to a brook and going up to Hognaston, a fascinating village with a church which is well worth visiting. At B5035 turn right past Carsington Reservoir site, and just beyond Hopton turn right for Kirk Ireton, another picturesque village. Descend to B5023, turn right and soon afterwards left to climb to Shottle. For a while the tall masts on the summit of Alport Height are visible ahead and to the left, and although not forming part of this route make an admirable landmark.

This section should gladden the heart of any country lover, and it is worth driving very slowly to appreciate just how delectable is this 'forgotten' gritstone region of Derbyshire. Descend to Belper Lane End and bear right in the village to go straight across A517, and keep to the right so as to curve round the village of Hazlewood. At the crossroads here turn right for Shottlegate—the reason for the deviation being to pass the impressive-looking Shottle Hall on the right. Again go straight across the A517, turning left at the next junction and then right at B5023; a mile later go left, and once more drive along country byways through Highcliffe Lane before turning sharp right into Ireton Wood. This village is an unspoilt gem. The imposing wrought-iron gates of Ireton Wood House are passed on the way towards Kirk Ireton, and at the 'Y'-junction a mile later, near a 795 feet high hill, 'The Mountain', turn left to descend to Millington Green. Unless it is particularly desired to visit Biggin, bear left and left again to Wardgate.

Cross the A517 and follow the country lane to Muggington Lane End, bearing right at the next junction to pass through Muggington. A little further down, turn right for Mercaston,

The Old and the New—54 Miles

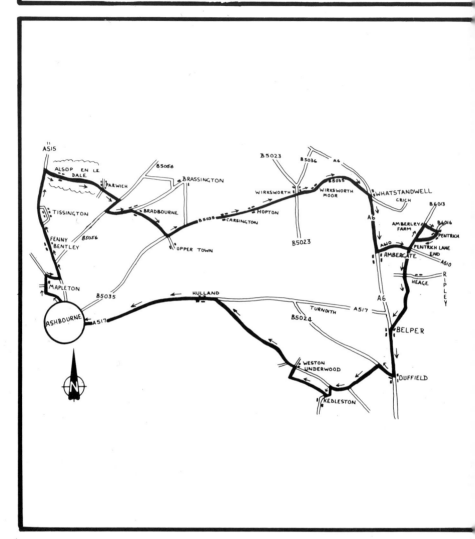

perimeter of Derby is now about to be pierced. Join the A6 in Belper, and continue through Duffield to turn right along the B5023 Wirksworth road before forking left after almost a mile.

The road passes Kedleston Hall, the home of Viscount Scarsdale and designed in 1757 by Robert Adam. He had just returned from an extensive tour of Italy, and thus was able to apply much of his acquired knowledge to the design. The marble hall with its columns of pink marble is an unforgettable sight, while the church and grounds are also worthy of exploration. Follow the country lanes to Weston Underwood and on to Hulland Ward, where merge with the A517. Turn left to return to Ashbourne, the extensive view on the right at the approach to the town making a suitable end to the route.

15: THE OLD AND THE NEW

Based on Ashbourne.

ROUTE: *Ashbourne—Mapleton—Fenny Bentley—Alsop-en-le-Dale— Parwich— Bradbourne—Carsington—Hopton—Wirksworth—Wirksworth Moor—Whatstandwell— Ambergate—Pentrich Lane End—Amberley Farm—Pentrich—Belper—Duffield— Kedleston—Weston Underwood—Hulland—Ashbourne.*

DISTANCE: *54 miles.*

MAPS: *1:50,000 O.S. Sheet No. 119—Buxton, Matlock and Dove Dale. Bartholomew National Map Series (1:100,000) No. 24—Derby and Nottingham.*

SOME of the prettiest villages of mid-Derbyshire are visited on this run, despite its skirting industrial towns on the fringe of Derby. Several churches with many historical treasures, the site of a revolution, and a Hall of magnificent proportions are memorable features to be seen. Before leaving Ashbourne visit the parish church of St. Oswald, a popular photographic subject from the outside and having an interior full of splendours. The pillar in the nave with the 'green man' peeping through the foliage and the alabaster tombs in the Boothby Chapel are two of the many treasures.

Turn left out of the Market Place past the Public Conviences on your right, onto a minor road, from which can be seen Thorpe Cloud and the beginnings of Dovedale. It leads to Mapleton, which has an unusual church to St. Mary with a pillared porch and a dome. Keep straight on, and at the 'T'-junction before Spendlane Farm turn right to rejoin A515, where go left to follow the main road for the next five miles. The first village encountered is Fenny Bentley, where the church on the left has an alabaster tomb to Thomas Beresford. Four miles further on, turn right onto the minor road to Alsop-en-le-Dale, a little hamlet which sets the mood for the next few miles. Pass through Parwich, a pleasant limestone village with several Halls on its perimeter and a church with a tall spire in the centre.

Bear right at all junctions until meeting the B5056, where turn right and soon afterwards left for Bradbourne. Even from the main road this village looks inviting, with its turreted church surrounded by trees, but once there the scene is unforgettable. The church has many fascinating features: an excellent example of a Norman archway, a Saxon cross in the churchyard, and, inside, a stone coffin and a gravestone of 1643. Take the right-hand fork at the 'Y'-junction, passing Netherton Hall on the left before meeting the B5035, where turn left. Pass through Carsington and Hopton to Wirksworth—Hopton Hall being the former home of Sir John Gell, whose tomb is in Wirksworth Church. Ascend to Wirksworth Moor and onto Whatstandwell on the B5035. Turn right on meeting the A6.

At Ambergate turn left along A610, and at Pentrich Lane End fork left to Amberley Farm on the B6013. On reaching the crossroads just north of the farm, turn right into Pentrich, the centre of a revolution in 1817. Although it never fully matured, the three ring-leaders were soon afterwards hanged, drawn and quartered in Derby to deter other such uprisings. Descend by turning right through the village and, on again reaching Pentrich Lane End, go to the right and almost immediately left for the B6013. On the right is an impressive windmill. Since Ambergate the scenery has changed to gritstone, and the industrial

43

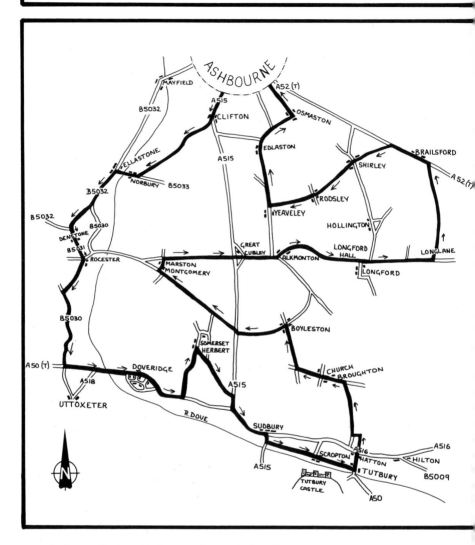

Longford is reached 2 miles later with Longford Hall, an imposing Georgian mansion which holds one spellbound with its long frontage, tall chimneys and the gardens and lake at the front. Beside the Hall is the church of St. Chad, noted for its tombs of the Longford family. Continue towards Derby for about three miles, turning left at Long Lane and then left again in three miles on meeting the A52, so as to pass through Brailsford. A mile further on branch left for Shirley, re-entering an area of country lanes and picturesque villages. Pass through Rodsley, Yeaveley and Edlaston before bearing right at a 'Y'-junction. One soon arrives at Osmaston, a jewel of Derbyshire with its thatched cottages and delightful surroundings. Continue along the minor road, which in due course merges with the A5 to reach Ashbourne.

16: CHURCHES AND DOVELAND

Based on Ashbourne.

ROUTE: *Ashbourne—Clifton—Norbury—Ellastone—Somersall Herbert—Sudbury—Scropton—Tutbury—Hatton—Church Broughton—Boyleston—Marston Montgomery—Great Brailsford—Shirley—Rodsley—Yeaveley—Edlaston—Osmaston—Ashbourne.*

DISTANCE: *60 miles.*

MAPS: *1:50,000 O.S. Sheet No. 128—Derby and Burton-upon-Trent. Bartholomew National Series (1:100,000)—No. 24—Derby and Nottingham.*

The area between Ashbourne and Burton-upon-Trent is rich in its church architecture and historical remains, and an additional interest is the River Dove, which here forms the Derbyshire boundary. Follow the A515 Lichfield road to Clifton, turning right beside the church and proceeding along a country lane with the Dove on the right. At Norbury turn right onto B5033, and immediately on the right is the church of St. Mary and St. Barlock. The beautiful setting, with a mediaeval Hall beside the church, sets the pace for the whole route; inside the church are several shafts of Saxon crosses, and two alabaster tombs of the Fitzherberts.

Continue towards Ellastone, and at the junction with the B5032 turn left to enter Staffordshire for a short distance. In Denstone go to the left along the B5031 to skirt Rocester, and continue on the B5030; on meeting the A50 on the outskirts of Uttoxeter turn left and re-enter Derbyshire by the Dove Bridge. Soon turn right into the charming village of Dovebridge, where legend holds that Robin Hood and Maid Marian were married under the 1,400-years-old yew tree guarding the entrance to the church of St. Cuthbert. In the church it is worth seeing the 17th Century deed box with three different locks; before it can be opened the vicar and the two church wardens must be present, for each has one of the keys. Rejoin the A50, and shortly afterwards turn left for Somersall Herbert, where be prepared for a surprise. Beside the church on the left stands an example of an Elizabethan mansion, which is so perfect that one feels one has stepped into a different century! Turn right and descend the hill, veering right opposite Sudbury Prison and soon afterwards left onto the A50 and into Sudbury. On the outskirts of the village on the right is the impressive Sudbury Hall, now under the care of the National Trust.

Fork right along A515 before turning left on the country lane to Scropton. Past here on the right can be seen Tutbury Castle, mentioned in run No 13 and worth a visit, if only for the view from the battlements of the meandering Dove. The church beside the entrance to the castle is an interesting Norman building, and near its main entrance is a pair of wooden stocks. Descend to Hatton, where go straight across the A516, and after a third of a mile turn left at the 'T'-junction to follow the country lane into Church Broughton. Continue on through Boyleston to Marston Montgomery, where the church of St. Giles is 11th Century and makes a contrast to the others seen on this route. Turn right for Great Cubley, and beyond to another fascinating church at Alkmonton. Its exterior walls are covered with a mass of beach pebbles.

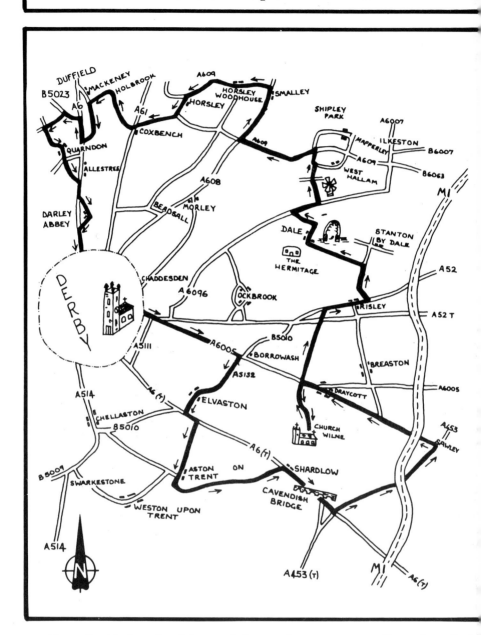

outside, and inside the colourful stained-glass windows consist not of figures but of little squares. Very little remains of the actual Abbey, which was one of the richest in Derbyshire but in Darley Street close to the river are some ruins, believed to have been a guest house or barn. The Boar's Head Mill is opposite, and a drive of a little over a mile leads back into central Derby.

17: AROUND THE CAPITAL

Based on Derby.

ROUTE: *Derby—Borrowash—Elvaston—Aston-on-Trent—Shardlow—Cavendish Bridge—Sawley—Draycott—Church Wilne—Risley—Stanton by Dale—Dale—West Hallam—Smalley—Horsley Woodhouse—Horsley— Coxbench—Holbrook—Mackeney—Duffield—Quarndon—Allestree—Darley Abbey—Derby.*

DISTANCE: *51 miles.*

MAPS: *1:50,000 O.S. Sheet Nos. 128—Derby and Burton-upon-Trent. 129—Nottingham and Loughborough. Bartholomew National Series (1:100,000)— No. 24—Derby and Nottingham.*

This run is purposefully short, for there is so much to visit and see near the capital of the county. Leave Derby on the A52 Nottingham road, bearing right some 2½ miles from the centre to follow the A6005 into Borrowash. On the outskirts of this village turn right along A5132, catching a glimpse of Elvaston Castle on the right, which is now a Country Park, before passing Elvaston and then Thurlston to meet the A6. Turn left, and shortly afterwards right, for Aston on Trent, from where continue along the road running parallel with the Trent and Mersey Canal before again joining the A6 to enter Shardlow. This is a most attractive village, especially its older quarter with the canal and Trent forming a popular weekend meeting place. Cross the Cavendish Bridge, and at the roundabout go left along the A453 into Sawley where turn left for Draycott.

In Draycott again turn left and go along beside the River Derwent to Church Wilne, where a font made from a pre-Norman cross is an unusual feature of the church. Return to Draycott, crossing the A6005, and beyond the A52 turn right into Risley. Half a mile past the Elizabethan church turn left for the minor road to picturesque Stanton by Dale, here going left for Dale—fully described in run No 13. Continue along the minor road to the A6096, where turn right; then left past a windmill on your right, complete with wooden sails. It is a splendid example, and although used by a manufacturing organisation it can be admired at first hand by walking up the track.

Continue towards West Hallam, and on to the A609 north of the village; ahead is Mapperley and Shipley Park. Turn left along the A609 and at the junction with the A608, turn right for Smalley, entering the village along A608 and in the centre going left on to A609 for Horsley Woodhouse. Once past here turn left for Horsley, but instead of going into this village bear left and then right, descending to cross the A61 at Coxbench. Bear right in front of a Hall and ascend to Holbrook, turning left to drive round the perimeter of Holbrook Hall before dropping down Duffield Bank to the A6 opposite Duffield Hall. Go to the left, and in just over a mile turn right for Quarndon, which has a long history and is closely connected with Kedleston three miles away. There used to be a cannon here which was a relic of the Civil War; it came in handy a hundred years later, when a group of rioters approached but then dispersed when they remembered the cannon!

Return the same way for a short distance before turning right, and after half a mile left, for Allestree, where a walk through Allestree Park with its lake can make a pleasing diversion. Before returning to Derby visit Darley Abbey; the church has a stone coffin

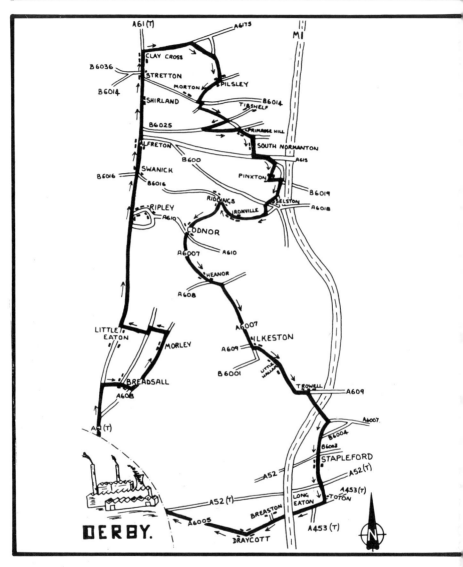

and at the intersection with B6016 turn right and into Ironville and Riddings, where i is interesting to take the minor road past the church.

Turn left, and drive via Golden Valley into Codnor, joining the A6007 for Heanor, a expanding industrial community, and Ilkeston, the third largest town in Derbyshire, o your left is the Erewash Valley and canal. Keep to the A6007, passing Trowell. Turn righ onto the B6003 through Stapleford to Toton and the A453. Turn right and right again ont the A6005 through Breaston. After another six miles this tour of the 'working' part of th country concludes with the return to Derby.

18: INDUSTRIAL DERBYSHIRE

Based on Derby.

ROUTE: Derby—Breadsall—Morley—Little Eaton—Ripley—Swanwick—Alfreton—Shirland—Stretton—Clay Cross—Pilsley—Morton—Primrose Hill—South Normanton—Pinxton—Selston—Riddings—Codnor—Heanor—Ilkeston—Little Hallam—Trowell—Stapleford—Toton—Long Eaton—Breaston—Derby.

DISTANCE: 64 miles.

MAPS: 1:50,000 O.S. Sheet Nos. 119—Buxton, Matlock and Dove Dale. 128—Derby and Burton-upon-Trent. 129—Nottingham and Loughborough. 120—Mansfield and the Dukeries. Bartholomew National Series—(1:100,000) No. 24—Derby and Nottingham.

ALTHOUGH this route basically goes through the industrial sector of Derbyshire, it includes several places of staggering beauty. One passes farms and churches full of fascinating historical remains and, despite passing through 'black' areas, the run should be just as memorable as one in the Peak District. Naturally there is only one day to do it—Sunday! Before starting, a visit to the old Silk Mill beside the Derwent is of considerable interest, for it now houses an Industrial Museum.

Leave Derby by the A61, and after two miles turn right into unspoilt Breadsall with its perfect example of an Elizabethan house. Continue along the lane to the A608, turning left, and just over a mile later reaching Morley, where descend the lane on your right to the church of St. Matthew. As already noted in the Dale Abbey section of run No 13, the four stained-glass windows form one of the wonders of Derbyshire. Go up the road to the junction at Morley Smithy, turning left and half a mile later left again, before going right to descend into Little Eaton. Join the A61 and stay on this road all the way to Clay Cross (17 miles).

The first major town is Ripley, where the large factory of Butterley on the town's outskirts has played a considerable part in the local life since 1792. Swanwick, with the Hayes forming a popular conference centre, is followed by Alfreton, from where the tall monument at Crich can be seen on the left. Follow a short stretch of dual carriageway, climbing to Fourlane Ends and bearing right towards Shirland, where the road misses the village but passes the church of St. Leonard with its recently-made stained-glass windows. Just north of here there is a spectacular view on the left over to Ogston Reservoir and the impressive Ogston Hall, and there is a further panorama on the right over industrial and agricultural Derbyshire on nearing Clay Cross. Turn right along the A6175 North Wingfield road, and after 1½ miles go to the right opposite a church into Waterloo. The next ten miles are on country lanes, passing farmland as well as slag heaps and mines.

From Pilsley turn right, but instead of going into Morton turn left on meeting B6014 and then right, and soon afterwards left, for B6025. At this junction bear right for Westhouses, and left into Primrose Hill. Here turn right at the crossroads in the middle of the village, and shortly go right again down Fordbridge Lane into South Normanton; then continue to Normanton Common and the A615. Turn right onto B6019 for Pinxton Green, where just in front of the bridge underneath the M1 bear right into Selston and Selston Green. The road passes the church of St. Helen's, which was founded in 1150. Cross the B600,

49

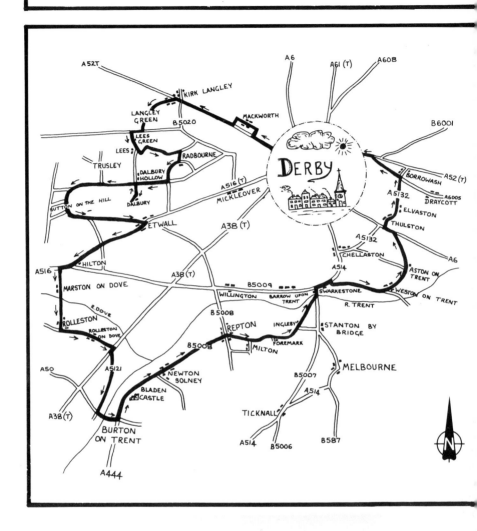

Trent & Mersey Canal

9: THE TRENT AND THE DOVE

Based on Derby.

ROUTE: *Derby—Mackworth—Langley Green—Lees Green—Radbourne—Dalbury—Etwall—Hilton—Marston on Dove—Dove Cliff—Burton on Trent—Bladen Castle—Newton Solney—Repton—Milton—Foremark—Ingleby—Swarkestone—Weston upon Trent—Aston upon Trent—Elvaston—Borrowash—Derby.*

DISTANCE: *50 miles.*

MAPS: *1:50,000 O.S. Sheet Nos. 128—Derby and Burton upon Trent. 129—Nottingham and Loughborough. Bartholomew National Series (1:100,000) No. 24—Derby and Nottingham.*

This is a run into the very heart of the southern region of Derbyshire, passing numerous historical remains and going along country lanes and main roads beside the Rivers Dove and Trent. From the centre of Derby take the A52 Ashbourne road, and on the outskirts of the city turn right to escape from the noise of modern travel by entering Mackworth. The first item to catch the eye is the church, which stands back from the road in a truly delightful setting. A little further along the lane on the right is the ivy-clad archway of Mackworth Castle, all that remains of a building believed to have been destroyed in the Civil War. Continue along the lane, rejoining the A52 and turning right to pass a farm wall on which the owner has mounted ploughs and wheels painted in bright colours.

At Kirk Langley turn left into the lane beside the church, which has many historical features, including graves of the Mayhill family dating back to 1600. On entering Langley Green there is an extensive view ahead over much of the southern sector of Derbyshire. On reaching the 'T'-junction just south of the village turn right, and half a mile later left, into the red-bricked village of Lees Green. At Lees bear left to pass on the right the tall Radbourne Hall standing amid woodland. A close view of this majestic building can be obtained by turning right to drive round the perimeter of the park. At the crossroads at Correl Hays turn right again to Dalbury Hollow, where go left at another crossroads and drop down to the 'no through road' to visit Dalbury Church. It is entered by walking under an archway of yew; notice that the font has some delightfully quaint and intricate carving. A piece of 13th Century stained glass and the petite battlemented tower are other noteworthy features.

After returning to Dalbury Hollow turn left, and at the junction just before Land Ends again turn left and curve round close to Sutton-on-the-Hill to turn right at the A516 in Etwall. At Etwall a block of almshouses stands next to the church, which contains the tomb of Sir John Port, founder of Repton School. It is also renowned for the two small oblong stained-glass windows above the altar, which are unique in church architecture and are believed to be 17th Century. Continue along the A516 through Hilton, turning left into Marston on Dove, another quiet corner, where carry straight on over the railway crossing and on to Dove Bridge. It is worth stopping here for a moment to watch the river meander down the picturesque valley. Turn left to Rolleston, keeping to the outskirts of the village and passing through Rolleston-on-Dove to reach the A5121, which should be followed for two miles before branching left along the A50 into Burton upon Trent.

Cross the Trent and turn left along B5008, which follows the river for much of the way. On entering Newton Park, Bladen Castle—the only brick castle in Derbyshire—is hidden among the trees, and past the drive entrance on the descent towards Newton Solney is a panoramic view on the left over towards the confluence of the Rivers Dove and Trent and across to Derby. At Repton one should visit the school and the church, where the Saxton crypt is a 'must'. Bear right beside the market cross, proceeding through Milton and passing on the right the impressive wrought-iron gates of Foremark Hall, now the Repton Preparatory School. Continue to Ingleby and Swarkestone; the route is particularly enjoyable as it runs alongside the Trent. Cross the river into Swarkestone, where turn right onto A514.

Go over the Trent and Mersey Canal, and turn right for Weston upon Trent and Aston upon Trent. The church here is fascinating; inside is a tombstone bearing the carved figures of a man and a woman, and also there is a basson, similar to the one at Beeley, which was used to accompany the hymns until the organ was installed. In the village turn left and drive to the A6, where go left and then right onto A5132 to pass Elvaston Castle on the left. At Borrowash join A6005, turn left, and in due course merge into the A52 to return to Derby.

Lock-Up—Smisby

52

20: THE SOUTHERN TIP

Based on Derby.

ROUTE: *Derby—Chellaston—Swarkestone—Stanton by Bridge—Melbourne—Ticknall—Smisby—Woodville—High Cross Bank—Overseal—Netherseal—Lullington—Coton in the Elms—Walton upon Trent—Roslington—Cauldwell—Swadlincote—Stanhope Bretby—Repton—Willington—Twyford—Stenson—Derby.*

DISTANCE: *57 miles.*

MAPS: *1:50,000 O.S. Sheet No. 128—Derby and Burton upon Trent. Bartholomew National Series (1:100,000)—No. 24—Derby and Nottingham.*

The southern tip of Derbyshire contains several historic villages and places of interest, which often amaze one for their scenic and idyllic qualities. Leave Derby by A514, passing through Chellaston and onto Swarkestone, where turn sharp left to cross the renowned Swarkestone Bridge. It is almost a mile long and mainly dates from the 18th Century, although parts go back another 400 years. The bridge saw some fierce fighting when Sir John Gell engaged the royalists in the Civil War. Proceed into Stanton by Bridge and left to reach Melbourne, a pretty village with a Hall which can be visited, a most interesting church and a tithe barn. In 1837 that giant of the outback, Melbourne in Australia, was named after the then Prime Minister of England, Viscount Melbourne, who in turn derived his title from this Derbyshire village. Hence it is today widely visited by Australians.

Continue to A514 in Ticknall—the church here is of note and closeby is Calke Abbey, National Trust property—turning left onto the B5006 for Smisby where the church has several tombs of the local Kendall family and village lockup closeby. Nearby is a tournament field, which is believed to have been the one used by Ivanhoe. Turn left in front of the church, and follow a country lane to Ann Well Place and the A50, where go right for Woodville. Bear left along A514 to High Cross Bank so as to see the mound where the fortress of Castle Gresley once stood. Fork left to follow A444, and two miles from Overseal turn right for Netherseal and the nearby River Mease. Go through the village heading once more for Overseal, but take the second left which passes the majestic grounds and Hall of Grangewood.

Turn left, and then follow the second left for Lullington, a quiet and pleasant village where the church has a beautiful stained glass window made in 1882 and forms an unforgettable sight with its maze of colouring. Turn right along the country road into Coton in the Elms, keeping left at the crossroads at Lads Grave to follow the county boundary and the river to Walton upon Trent. Turn right here, and soon afterwards left, for picturesque Roslington, and then branch left towards Linton before going left again in half a mile to enter the hamlet of Cauldwell. Fork right to head for B5005 and Swadlincote.

At Swadlincote follow the A50 Burton on Trent road, after 1½ miles turning right to pass the extensive earth works of a castle. Opposite those bear right and enter Bretby, where turn right and soon afterwards fork left at the 'T'-junction for Repton, one of the most prized possessions of Derbyshire. It has the famous Repton School and a market cross, but its finest asset is the church, which has one of the best examples in existence of a Saxon crypt. As

The Southern Tip—57 Miles

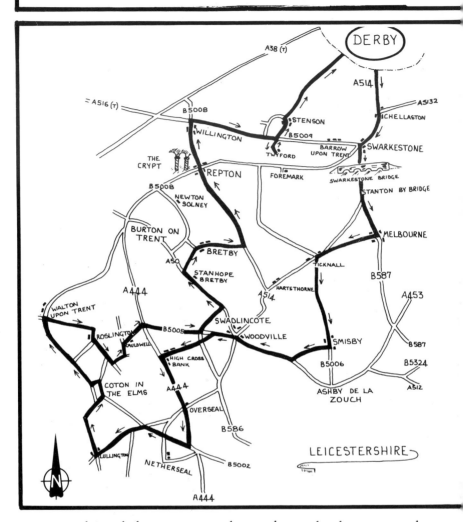

soon as one descends the stone steps and opens the wooden door, one somehow sen
that a rare piece of church architecture is about to be seen.

Cross the River Trent into Willington, turning right along A5132 and then right aga
into the delightful hamlet of Twyford. Here is a place which, with its peaceful River Tre
and an ivy-clad church, makes one forget time. The interior of the church is striking
Norman arch guarding the entrance to the chancel and a stained glass window behi
the latter letting a shaft of light enter the perfect scene. Return to A5132, crossing ov
and proceeding through Stenson into Derby. There are many places to visit here, but th
is one worthy of special mention—the Cathedral. Inside, look for the tomb of Bess
Hardwick, Elizabeth Cavendish, who, as already related, played an important and intrigui
part in Derbyshire history.

OTHER BOOKS
BY JOHN N.MERRILL
& PUBLISHED BY JNM PUBLICATIONS
DAY WALK GUIDES

)RT CIRCULAR WALKS IN THE PEAK DISTRICT Fifteen carefully selected walks—3 to 5 miles—starting
า a car park. The walks cover the variety of the area—the gritstone edges, limestone dales, and peat
orland. All follow well defined paths; include a pub for lunch; and are suitable for all the family. 44 pages
าaps 22 photographs ISBN 0 907496 37 7

ιK DISTRICT TOWN WALKS Twelve short circular walks around the principal towns and villages of the
k District. Including Castleton, Buxton, Hathersage, Eyam,Tissington and Ashbourne. Each walk has a
ıiled map and extensive historical notes complete with pictures. 60 pages 12 maps 96 photographs
ISBN 0 907496 20 2

ιK DISTRICT: LONG CIRCULAR WALKS Fifteen differing walks 12 to 18 miles long for the serious hiker.
ιy follow lesser used paths in the popular areas, giving a different perspective to familiar landmarks. 64
ιs 16 maps 28 photographs ISBN 0 907496 17 2

STERN PEAKLAND—CIRCULAR WALKS The first book to cover this remarkably attractive side of the
ional Park—west of Buxton. The guide combines both long and short walks. 25—3 to 11 mile long walks with
ɔmely detailed maps to help you explore the area. 48 pages 23 maps 22 photographs ISBN 0 907496 15 6

;HORT CIRCULAR WALKS AROUND MATLOCK 12 walks of about 4 miles long into the Matlock area
in history and folklore and make ideal family outings. Included is an 'alpine' walk, using Matlock Bath's
e car as part of the route. 52 pages 44 photographs 12 maps ISBN 0 907496 25 3

)RT CIRCULAR WALKS IN THE DUKERIES More than 25 walks in the Nottinghamshire/Sherwood Forest
, past many of the historic buildings that make up the Dukeries area. 56 pages 40 photographs 21 maps
ISBN 0 907496 29 6

ιAL WALKS VOL.1—DERBYSHIRE AND NOTTINGHAMSHIRE More than 30 walks both short and
along the canals in the area—Cromford, Erewash, Chesterfield, Derby, Trent & Mersey,Nottingham,
ton and Nutbrook canals. 84 pages 60 photographs 32 maps ISBN 0 907496 30 X

E TO BE FIT...STROLLING WITH JOHN John Merrill's personal guide to walking in the countryside to
fit and healthy. He describes what equipment to use, where to go, how to map read, use a compass and
t to do about blisters! 36 pages 23 photos 2 sketches 3 charts ISBN 0 907496 19 9

CHALLENGE WALKS

IN MERRILL'S PEAK DISTRICT CHALLENGE WALK A 25 mile circular walk from Bakewell, across
ys and heights involving 3,700 feet of ascent. More than 2,000 people have already completed the walk.
dge and completion certificate is available to those who complete. 32 pages 18 photographs 9 maps
ISBN 0 907496 18 0

'N MERRILL'S YORKSHIRE DALES CHALLENGE WALK A 23 mile circular walk from Kettlewell in the
t of the Dales. The route combines mountain, moorlands, limestone country and dale walking with 3,600
ɔf ascent. A badge and certificate is available to those who complete the route. 32 pages 16 photographs
ps ISBN 0 907496 28 8

'N MERRILL'S NORTH YORKSHIRE MOORS CHALLENGE WALK A 24 mile circular walk from
'hland in the heart of the moors. The route combines moorland, river valley and coastal walking and uses
ι Hood's Bay as the half way point. Involves 2,000 feet of ascent and a badge and certificate is available
ɔse who complete. 32 pages 18 photographs 9 maps ISBN 0 907496 36 9

RIVER'S WAY A two day walk of 43 miles, down the length of the Peak District National Park. Inaugurated
'reated by John, the walk starts at Edale, the end of the Pennine Way, and ends at Ilam. Numerous hostels,
ιgrounds,B&B, and pubs lie on the route, as you follow the five main river systems of the Peak—Noe,
'ent, Wye, Dove, and Manifold. 52 pages 35 photographs 7 maps ISBN 0 907496 08 3

PEAK DISTRICT: HIGH LEVEL ROUTE A hard 90 mile, weeks walk, around the Peak District, starting fr Matlock. As the title implies the walk keeps to high ground while illustrating the dramatic landscape of the Pe District. The walk was inaugurated and created by John and is used by him for training for his major walks! pages 31 photographs 13 maps ISBN 0 907496 1(

PEAK DISTRICT MARATHONS The first reference book to gather together all the major and classical lo walks of the Peak District between 25 and 50 miles long. Many are challenge walks with badges and complet cards for those who complete. The longest walk—280 miles—inaugurated by John is around the en Derbyshire boundary. Each walk has a general map, accommodation list, and details of what guides and m are needed. 56 pages 20 photographs 20 maps ISBN 0 907496 1

HISTORICAL GUIDES

WINSTER—A VISITOR'S GUIDE A detailed look at a former lead mining community which still retain Morris dancing team and annual pancake races. A two mile walk brings you to many historical buildi including the 17th century Market House. Illustrated by old photographs. 20 pages 21 photographs 1 m ISBN 0 907496 2

DERBYSHIRE INNS The first book to tell the story behind more than 150 inns in the Peak District and Derbysl area. With details of legends, murders and historical anecdotes, the book gives added pleasure or impetu explore the pubs of the region. Profusely illustrated with 65 photographs and a brief history of brewin Derbyshire. 68 pages 57 photographs 5 maps ISBN 0 907496 1

100 HALLS AND CASTLES OF THE PEAK DISTRICT AND DERBYSHIRE A visitor's guide to the princ historical buildings of the region. Many are open to the public and the guide describes the history of the build from the Domesday Book to the present time. The book is illustrated by 120 photographs and makes an excel souvenir gift of one of England's finest architectural areas. 120 pages 116 photographs 4 maps ISBN 0 907496 2

TOURING THE PEAK DISTRICT AND DERBYSHIRE Twenty circular routes of about 50 miles for the motc or cyclist. Each route has a set theme, such as the gritstone edges or in the steps of Mary, Queen of Sc Deatiled maps for each route and fifty photographs make this a useful companion to the P District/Derbyshire area. 76 pages 45 photographs 20 maps ISBN 0 907496 2

JOHN'S MARATHON WALKS

EMERALD COAST WALK The story of John's walk up the total length of the west coast of Ireland exploration of more than fifty islands—1,600 miles. 132 pages 32 photographs 12 maps ISBN 0 907496 0

TURN RIGHT AT LAND'S END In 1978 John Merrill became the first person to walk the entire coastlin Britain—6,824 miles in ten months. The book details the route, how he ascended our three major mountains how he found a wife. Included are more than 200 photographs he took on the walk, which is also a uni guide to our coastline. 246 pages 214 photographs 10 maps ISBN 0 907496 2

WITH MUSTARD ON MY BACK John has gathered together the stories of his first decade walking—1970-1980. Here is a collection of unique walks in Britain, from a 2,000 mile walk linking the National Parks of England and Wales together to a 450 mile walk from Norwich to Durham. ISBN 0 907496 2

TURN RIGHT AT DEATH VALLEY During the summer of 1984, John walked coast to coast across Amer a distance of 4,226 miles in 177 days. Few have walked across and none have taken so difficult a route. crossed all the main mountain ranges, climbed 14,000 foot mountains, crossed deserts in 100 degrees, wa rim to rim of the Grand Canyon in 8½ hours, and crossed the famed Death Valley. The walk is without par and the story is the remarkable tale of this unique adventure. ISBN 0 907496 2

FORTHCOMING TITLES—

SHORT CIRCULAR WALKS IN THE STAFFORDSHIRE MOORLANDS
ARKWRIGHT OF CROMFORD
CANAL WALKS VOL.2—DERBYSHIRE, CHESHIRE AND STAFFORDSHIRE
CANAL WALKS VOL.3—DERBYSHIRE, LEICESTERSHIRE AND LINCOLNSHIRE
THE LITTLE JOHN CHALLENGE WALK